S0-BNB-694

SUCCESS
MASTERY

Most CelebrityPress® titles are available at special quantity discounts for bulk purchases for sales promotions, premiums, fundraising, and educational use. Special versions or book excerpts can also be created to fit specific needs.

For more information, please write:
CelebrityPress®
520 N. Orlando Ave, #2
Winter Park, FL 32789
or call 1.877.261.4930

Visit us online at: www.CelebrityPressPublishing.com

SUCCESS
MASTERY

CelebrityPress®
Winter Park, Florida

CONTENTS

CHAPTER 1

MASTERING THE ART OF SUCCESS

BY JACK CANFIELD

It's often been said that success is a team sport. It's not just what you know, it's also who you know. And while you may be able to create tremendous success on your own, traveling the path of success with others makes the journey more enjoyable. Plus, the added accountability will propel you to success faster (and further) than you originally envisioned.

In my career, success in any undertaking has come down to not just who I know—but also who I have on my team. Along the way, I've learned a number of success principles that can now help you build your own network of influencers, mentors and experts—and develop a support team of people who can help you succeed.

BUILD YOUR PERSONAL NETWORK OF INFLUENCERS AND EXPERTS BY DEVELOPING GENUINE RELATIONSHIPS

One of the most important skills for success in today's world, especially for entrepreneurs and business owners, is networking. Jim Bunch, the creator of the Ultimate Game of Life, once stated,

11

"Your network will determine your net worth." In my life, this has proven to be true. The more time I have spent consciously building and nurturing my network of advisers, colleagues, clients, students and fans, the more successful I have become.

Businesses and careers are built on relationships, and relationships form when people meet and interact with each other over time in an authentic and caring way. As I'm sure you're aware, statistics confirm over and over that people prefer to do business with people they know, respect and trust.

Effective networking, therefore, is all about developing relationships.

Your goal for networking

In developing your own personal network, your job is to seek out people who know what you don't—and who can help you connect where you can't. Initially, your goal shouldn't be to make a sale, but instead to seek advice, connections, recommendations and insights. To the extent that you can provide something in return, do so. But remember that developing genuine relationships that you can call upon at any time—for years into the future, potentially—takes time and consideration. It requires careful thought and a mindfulness for others.

My good friend Ivan Misner, founder of the international networking phenomenon BNI Worldwide, explains that good networking is a combination of three things: visibility, credibility and profitability.

Visibility is you and another individual becoming aware of each other. The individual—who may be a source of information, referrals to people who can help you or even a potential customer—may learn about you through your public relations, social media or advertising efforts—or through someone you both know. Soon, you might become personally acquainted and communicate on a first-name basis. That's visibility.

Credibility means you take the next step and become reliable and worthy of the other person's confidence. You begin to form expectations of each other and those expectations are fulfilled. Credibility increases when appointments are kept, promises are acted upon, facts are verified, and services are rendered. The old saying, Results speak louder than words, is true. Credibility also comes from third parties. Will someone they know vouch for you? Are you honest? Is your project or business legitimate? Are you effective? Are you someone who can be counted on in a crunch? If you are, your credibility will grow—as will important and beneficial relationships.

Profitability is what comes from mature relationships (business or personal) that are mutually rewarding and where both people gain something from the connection. This stage may be reached quickly—such as when an urgent need arises—or it may take years. Most likely, it's somewhere in between. Of course, much depends on the quality of your interaction with each other— but most especially on the desire of both parties to move the relationship forward.*

My closest and most productive network

Of course, profiting from relationships isn't limited to making money from a new customer or getting a referral. It may come in the form of a connection to someone who can help you launch a new initiative or otherwise grow your business. It may include access to a mentor or a professional adviser or a contact in another industry who can help you expand your market. It might be the ability to delegate more of your workload, gain substantial free time for your hobby or personal interests—or spend more quality time with your family.

My closest and most productive network has included my business partner Patty Aubery, and my *Success Principles* coauthor Janet

Switzer—two women who've not only been close friends and colleagues for 25 years, but who have also developed a robust and influential network from which I've benefitted. By combining their own contact list with people I know, we've generated millions of dollars in business, accumulated a million Facebook fans, and produced millions of customers, clients and students who follow *The Success Principles*. Our combined contact lists are filled with hundreds of key individuals who can help out with advice, direction, a name, an idea, resources, marketing assistance and more. At any time, we can ask each other, *Who do we know who can help with this new initiative?* —confident that we can get our needs and wants addressed within days. That's the real "profitability" of a network.

FORM A MASTERMIND GROUP TO KEEP YOU FOCUSED, ENTHUSIASTIC AND INNOVATIVE

One of the most powerful tools for success ever identified is a process called *masterminding*. We all know that two heads are better than one when it comes to solving a problem or creating a result. So, imagine having a permanent group of five to six people who meet regularly for the purpose of problem-solving, brainstorming, networking, encouraging and motivating each other.

Napoleon Hill first wrote about mastermind groups in 1937 in his classic book *Think and Grow Rich*. All the world's richest industrialists—from the early 20th Century to today's modern icons of business—have harnessed the power of the mastermind group. In fact, it's the one concept achievers reference most when they credit any one thing with helping them become successful.

Millions have discovered that a mastermind group can focus special energy on your efforts—in the form of knowledge, new ideas, introductions, a vast array of resources, and, most important, spiritual energy. It's this spiritual aspect that Napoleon Hill wrote about extensively. He said that if we are in tune with the mastermind—that is, God, Source, the universal power, Infinite Intelligence—we have significantly more positive energy available to us, a power that can be focused on our success.

How a mastermind group works

A mastermind group is made up of people who come together on a regular basis—weekly, biweekly, or monthly—to share ideas, thoughts, information, feedback, contacts, and resources. By getting the perspective, knowledge, experience, and resources of others in the group, not only can you greatly expand your own limited view of the world, you can also advance your own goals and projects more quickly.

A mastermind group can be composed of people from your own industry or profession—or people from different walks of life. It can focus on business issues, personal issues or both. But for a mastermind group to be powerfully effective, people must be comfortable enough with each other to tell the truth. Some of the most valuable feedback I have ever received has come from members of my mastermind group confronting me about overcommitting, selling my services too cheaply, focusing on the trivial, not delegating enough, thinking too small, and playing it safe.

If you're not in a mastermind group already, I recommend that you form one (or join one) as soon as possible.*

Mastermind groups nurture new ideas and initiatives In 2010, Jill Douka of Athens, Greece left my Breakthrough to Success training with the commitment to be part of a mastermind group with five other attendees from different countries. When the economic downturn in Greece began affecting her local network, Jill looked forward to meeting with her global mastermind group on Skype and Google Hangouts—spending an hour every other week using words other than default, unemployment and debt.

Before long, Jill learned through her mastermind group about TED talks and gave her first international speech in Chennai, India. On the plane trip home, an idea took shape in her mind: what if instead of just one TED talk, Jill created positive-focused, interactive events—then made videos of them available on YouTube so people around the world could benefit?

While civil unrest and economic problems in Greece made Jill hesitant to discuss her idea with colleagues in Athens, her mastermind group was enthusiastic. With their constant encouragement and support, Jill held the first one-day workshop in Athens to a jam-packed audience of 500 attendees and 300 livestream participants—all supported by 70 volunteers and 57 corporate sponsors. The feedback was tremendous. The following November, Sergio Sedas—another of my graduates—produced the second such event in Mexico—with more than 4,000 people participating in interactive solution-focused workshops given by presenters from the United States, Mexico, Canada, and Bermuda.

What could a mastermind group do for you?

FIND A MENTOR AND FOLLOW THEIR ADVICE

Another key strategy that successful people use is to constantly seek out experts in their field for advice, direction and information. The truth is there are *countless* people who've triumphed over the specific hardship you're facing—or who have succeeded in your specific area of endeavor. Why not take advantage of all that wisdom and experience by finding a mentor who has already been down the road you want to travel?

All you have to do is ask.

It's easier than you think

While it may seem daunting at first to contact successful people and ask for ongoing advice and assistance, it's easier than you think to enlist the mentorship of those who are far ahead of you in the areas in which you'd like to succeed.

What mentors do more than anything, says famed speaker and bestselling author Les Brown, is help you see possibilities. In other words, mentors help you overcome "possibility blindness" both by acting as a role model for you and by conveying a certain level of expectation as they communicate with you.

When Les started his speaking career in the early 1980s, he sent a cassette tape of his earliest keynote speech to the late Dr. Norman Vincent Peale, the world-renowned speaker and publisher of *Guideposts* magazine. That cassette tape led to a long and fruitful relationship for Les, as Dr. Peale not only took Les under his wing and counseled him on his speaking style, but also quietly opened doors and helped Les get important speaking engagements.

Perhaps like Les, you just need someone to open doors for you. Or perhaps you need a referral to a technical expert who can help you build a new service for your company. Maybe you simply need validation that the path you're pursuing is the right one. A mentor can help you with all of these things, but you need to be prepared to ask for specific advice.

Do your homework

One of the easiest ways to research the names and backgrounds of people who have been successful in your field is to read industry magazines, search the Internet, ask trade association executive directors, attend trade shows and conventions, call fellow entrepreneurs, or approach others who operate in your industry or profession.

Look for mentors who have the kind of well-rounded experience you need to tackle your goal. When you start seeing a pattern of the same few people being recommended, you know you've identified your short list of possible mentors.

The Success Principles coauthor Janet Switzer regularly mentors people on how to grow their small business. When Lisa Miller of CRA Management Group called Janet, she was just about to sign away a large percentage of her revenues to someone she thought would help her develop a new area of her business. Janet showed Lisa how to instantly accomplish the same goal without outside parties and even helped her land new business from existing clients, accelerating Lisa's company growth plan by four months and earning her hundreds of thousands of extra dollars.

To contact possible mentors like Janet and ensure a successful conversation once you do, make a list of specific points you'd like to cover in your first conversation, such as why you'd like them to mentor you and what kind of help you might be looking for. Be brief, but be confident, too.

The truth is that successful people like to share what they have learned with others. It's a human trait to want to pass on wisdom. Not everyone will take the time to mentor you, but many will if asked. You simply need to make a list of the people you would like to have as your mentor and ask them to devote a few minutes a month to you.

Some will say no, but some will say yes. Keep asking people until you get a positive response.

Follow their advice and return the favor

Mentors don't like to have their time wasted. So when you seek out their advice, follow it. Study their methods, ask your questions, make sure you understand the process—then, as much as is humanly possible, follow your mentor's suggestions. Try them on and see how they work for you. You can always adjust and improve upon them as you go along.

Be prepared to give your mentors something in return, too—even if it's something simple such as keeping them updated on industry information or calling with new opportunities that might benefit them. Look for ways to give back to your mentors. Help others, too. What a great reward to any mentor—to eventually have their former protégé out in the world mentoring others!

BUILD A POWERFUL TEAM THAT LETS YOU FOCUS ON YOUR CORE GENIUS

Every high achiever has a powerful team of key staff members, consultants, vendors, and helpers who do the bulk of the work while he or she is free to create new sources of income and new opportunities for success. The world's greatest philanthropists, athletes, entertainers, professionals, and others also have people who manage projects and handle everyday tasks—enabling them to do more for others, hone their craft, practice their sport and so on.

To help you clarify what you should be spending your time on and what you should be delegating to others, I recommend an exercise called *The Total Focus Process*. The goal is to find the top one, two or three activities that best use your core genius, bring you the most money, and produce the greatest level of enjoyment.

1. *Start by listing those activities that occupy your time,* whether they're business-related, personal or volunteer work. List even small tasks like returning phone calls, filing or photocopying.

2. *Choose from this list those one, two or three things* you're particularly brilliant at, your special talents—those unique things very few other people can do as well as you. Also choose from this list the three activities that generate *the most income* for you or your company. Any activities that you are brilliant at and that generate the most income for you or your company are activities you'll want to focus on.

3. *Finally, create a plan for delegating remaining activities to others.* Delegating takes time and training, but over time you can off-load the nonessential tasks on your list until you are doing less of the ones with little payoff—and more of what you're really good at. That is how you create a brilliant career.

Seek out key "staff" members and advisors

If you're a business owner or career professional, start training key people to take over the tasks you identified above. If you're a one-person business, start looking for a dynamic number-two person who could handle your projects, book your sales transactions, and completely take over other tasks while you concentrate on what you do best. If philanthropic pursuits or community projects are your "business," there are volunteers you can "hire" to help you—including college interns, who may work solely for class credit.

And if you are a stay-at-home parent, your most valuable "staff" will be your house cleaner, your babysitter and other people who can help you get away for time by yourself or with your spouse. A part-time helper can do grocery shopping, get your car washed, pick up the kids or pick up the dry cleaning—all for a modest wage. If you're a single parent, these folks are even more important to your successful future.

In addition to business and personal helpers, high achievers typically have a powerful team of *professional* advisors to turn to for support. Today's world is a complicated place. Professional advisors—such as your banker, your lawyers, a high-net-worth certified public accountant, your investment counselor, your doctor, nutritionist, personal trainer, and the leader of your religious organization—can walk you through challenges and opportunities, saving you time, effort and usually money. If you run a business, these advisors are essential.

BUILD A COMMUNITY AND PASS ON YOUR LEGACY

To truly master the art of success, you also need to pursue one more critical activity: building a community of followers who can join you in expanding your work, fulfilling your vision and—most importantly—securing your legacy.

Virtually all great thinkers of our age have managed to pass down their wisdom and life's work once they can no longer be active. Today, that "act of succession" is easier than ever.

The Internet and social media makes it possible

Today, social media has hit the tipping point where we're now seeing millions of followers convert into fellow devotees, passionate advocates, enthusiastic buyers, and committed partners for social change. Building a community of followers for your work or philanthropic pursuit guarantees there will be a network of people to join you in virtually any venture you want to pursue.

The key is to attract followers who will stay engaged with you and your message—then pass on your information to their own friends, colleagues and fans. To reach that goal, you'll want to maintain an ongoing presence on the most popular social media sites including Facebook, LinkedIn and Twitter.

While you can spend time writing your own posts and articles, then master the technology needed to "boost" your social media activity, I recommend you check out Social5Marketing.com, a done-for-you service that provides a team of world-class writers from top publications with smart online marketers to write, post and even run advertising for you on the major social-media platforms. Best of all, your online activity is scheduled, managed, executed and tracked for less than you'd pay your teenager. Whether you use this service (which also writes your blog, does email marketing and helps generate prospective buyers for your business or cause), you'll want to establish a personal brand, build your online presence, and pursue community building as an activity to ultimately support your success.

About Jack

Known as America's #1 Success Coach, Jack Canfield is the CEO of the Canfield Training Group in Santa Barbara, CA, which trains and coaches entrepreneurs, corporate leaders, managers, sales professionals and the general public in how to accelerate the achievement of their personal, professional and financial goals.

Jack Canfield is best known as the coauthor of the #1 New York Times bestselling *Chicken Soup for the Soul®* book series, which has sold more than 500 million books in 47 languages, including 11 New York Times #1 bestsellers. As the CEO of Chicken Soup for the Soul Enterprises he helped grow the Chicken Soup for the Soul® brand into a virtual empire of books, children's books, audios, videos, CDs, classroom materials, a syndicated column and a television show, as well as a vigorous program of licensed products that includes everything from clothing and board games to nutraceuticals and a successful line of Chicken Soup for the Pet Lover's Soul® cat and dog foods.

His other books include *The Success Principles™: How to Get from Where You Are to Where You Want to Be* (recently revised as the 10th Anniversary Edition), *The Success Principles for Teens, The Aladdin Factor, Dare to Win, Heart at Work, The Power of Focus: How to Hit Your Personal, Financial and Business Goals with Absolute Certainty, You've Got to Read This Book, Tapping into Ultimate Success, Jack Canfield's Key to Living the Law of Attraction,* and his recent novel—*The Golden Motorcycle Gang: A Story of Transformation.*

Jack is a dynamic speaker and was recently inducted into the National Speakers Association's Speakers Hall of Fame. He has appeared on more than 1000 radio and television shows including Oprah, Montel, Larry King Live, the Today Show, Fox and Friends, and two hour-long PBS Specials devoted exclusively to his work. Jack is also a featured teacher in 12 movies including *The Secret, The Meta-Secret, The Truth, The Keeper of the Keys, Tapping into the Source,* and *The Tapping Solution.*

Jack has personally helped hundreds of thousands of people on six different continents become multi-millionaires, business leaders, best-selling authors, leading sales professionals, successful entrepreneurs, and world-class athletes while at the same time creating balanced, fulfilling and healthy lives.

His corporate clients have included Virgin Records, SONY Pictures, Daimler-Chrysler, Federal Express, GE, Johnson & Johnson, Merrill Lynch, Campbell's Soup, Re/ Max, The Million Dollar Forum, The Million Dollar Roundtable, The Entrepreneur Organization, The Young Presidents Organization, the Executive Committee, and the World Business Council.

He is the founder of the Transformational Leadership Council and a member of Evolutionary Leaders, two groups devoted to helping create a world that works for everyone.

Jack is a graduate of Harvard, earned his M.Ed. from the University of Massachusetts and has received three honorary doctorates in psychology and public service. He is married, has three children, two step-children and a grandson.

For more information, visit:
- www.JackCanfield.com

CHAPTER 2

SEVEN ATTRIBUTES OF SUCCESS

BY LAURENCE J. (LARRY) PINO, ESQ.

I feel so very honored to collaborate with Jack Canfield and other colleagues in writing a chapter reflecting my views on the attributes of successful living in both business and in life. When I first got the call, it occurred to me that I might want to create some thoughts which have occurred to me of late, as to those things which have proven true for me.

However, in the midst of thinking it through, I remembered a talk I had done some time ago where I did my very best to summarize what I considered to be the rules or, said differently, the "Attributes of Success." As I read through the transcript of that particular lecture and put them side by side with what life has taught me in the years that passed, I realized how tried and true those things are which we need to do, in order to be successful in our lives. In short, while they can be refreshed with current events, they do remain unaffected by the passage of time.

So, in bringing them up-to-date for today in this particular book, I do hope they ring true to you.

What I am going to be covering are seven specific Attributes or

Rules which, quite honestly, are all that are necessary for you to be successful in business and in life.

I have two requests for you:

- My first request is that you simply suspend judgment until the chapter is finished.

- As for my second, as odd as it might sound, I would request you share this book (and this chapter) with your loved ones as you work through it, not only because your loved ones are important to you, but also because they're an important influence on your life. I want to share with them as much as I want to share with you what I consider to be the essential attributes for a successful attitude in this country. So, let me ask you to get your spouse or your significant other involved. Get your housemates involved and let's find out what it really means to become successful.

Let's get started. We're going to cover seven points for what I consider to be the perspective it takes to master success in this country. I hope to have converted you to a true believer by the end of the chapter.

I. Commitment to Professional Competency

The first Attribute of Success is the commitment to what I call *Professional Competency*. What do I mean by the *Commitment to Professional Competency*? When I discuss Professional Competency, what I'm talking about is the knowledge it takes to produce mastery of whatever business in which you're involved.

At this point in time, now that you are reading this book, you might be involved in any number of things. You might be involved in some network marketing program or multi-level marketing program. You might be involved in a part-time business. You might be involved in a full-time business. You may have a part-time or a full-time job. It doesn't matter what your background is, what you are doing, or how often you are doing it. The fact is that if you want to be successful in any type of business, particularly if you want it to be quantified by measurable performance, you have to master Professional Competency.

What does Professional Competency mean?

Professional Competency means mastering the tools for whatever self-employment trade you're doing. In my parlance, you need to know it like the back of your hand.

I've been involved in a number of different businesses over the years. In law school and for several years thereafter, I started and ran a publishing company called Intrelex Corporation. We did legal research and writing for lawyers and added several trade publications at McGraw-Hill over the five-year run.

I eventually sold the company to my partner. I then got involved in a sporting goods business with my dad and took a sporting goods business from one store to nine retail stores and then franchised those out. I followed that with a wholesale sporting goods operation which became the largest distributor of institutional athletic equipment in the state of Florida.

I was, and continue to remain, a practicing lawyer.

While running the sporting goods business and practicing law, I opened and operated seven different restaurants – seven restaurants! I had so many restaurants at a certain point that I told my friends if I ever did another restaurant to just shoot me, because I had obviously lost my mind.

And there were countless other businesses: as a matter of fact, eighty of them at last count. But here's the point. Whatever the business was – whatever the industry – the first and essential precondition for the business was what I call Professional Competency – knowing the business.

And the way I describe that best is that if you know the business like the back of your hand, nobody can compete against you effectively or can gain the upper hand (no pun intended).

Professional Competency involves two stages. The first stage of Professional Competency is learning the business right from the 'get-go' . . . right from the start. The second stage of Professional Competency is ongoing training: those people who are striving to know their business like the back of their hand are not satisfied with initial training, they want ongoing training. They can't get enough.

For every business in which I have been involved, I've always done three things. I always subscribed to every periodical I could read; I always read or listened to every book I could find; and I always went to all the conventions, conferences and symposia which were relevant. Simply put: the more you learn, the better and more competent you become.

I don't know your background, of course; I don't know your history and, candidly, it doesn't really matter.

If you allow yourself the opportunity to commit to knowing whatever business you do like the back of your hand, along with following the other attributes I lay out here, I want to suggest respectfully to you that you have every reason to believe you will be producing a six- to seven-digit income each year, if that happens to be your goal, or you will become a thought-leader in that space, if that is your objective.

So, the first Attribute of Success is a Commitment to Professional Competency – a commitment to learning a business like the back of your hand.

II. Commitment to Being Single-Minded of Purpose

The second commitment I want to see from you is a commitment not only to know a business and to learn a business like the back of your hand, but I also want to see what I call a commitment to being Single-Minded of Purpose.

When you read about billionaires in the newspapers buying up this or that company, I will guarantee you that not one of those billionaires started off that way. Where they started making their money was in a single business: one business, not a bunch of different businesses. You show me somebody who is successful in different businesses, and I'll show you somebody who became successful in just one.

You cannot be successful or make a lot of money by focusing on half a dozen different things. It's the old expression – a 'jack of all trades' is never a master of one. Indeed, a 'jack of all trades' is a master of none. The only way to make serious money – or seriously succeed – is to be Single-Minded of Purpose. Whatever that purpose is doesn't really matter.

I have a friend, for example, who has become very successful operating just one restaurant. And that's all he's done from the time he started off as a maître d' to the time he eventually became a chef to the time he began operating his very first restaurant (which was little more than a hole in a second-rate shopping center wall), to the next restaurant and to the next. From the time he was 17 years old up to today, operating an expensive restaurant which has become an institution earning him some $7 million in annual profit, this attribute paid off handsomely. He was Single-Minded of Purpose.

You don't have to start off at 17 years old. But you do have to have that Single-Mindedness of Purpose. I want to suggest to you that you take a look at everything you are doing and evaluate them in the context of this Attribute of Success.

I once got a call from a person who had taken a training program I conducted for the Cash Flow Industry I founded years earlier. He took my training program, bought my tapes, resource manuals and workbooks and he put them on the mantle. Of course, he didn't go out and work the business in any significant way.

He called me up some two months later and he said, "Larry, I was just so impressed with your tapes and with the Cash Flow System." And I said, "I really appreciate you calling and telling me that." He said, "Can I ask you something?" And he started talking to me about some multi-level long-distance telephone service he wanted to sell me. And I gently said, "You know my friend, we've got just about the cheapest telephone service I can imagine. We negotiate pretty well and we tend to know what we're doing. So, the chances are not real strong you're going to be able to offer a service to us that will make economic sense. But may I ask you something on a different topic? You bought into my Cash Flow System. You've listened to little of it and you haven't applied anything yet. So, where are you? What other things are you involved in?" And he started telling me about the fact that he was involved in this particular multi-level telephone service. He was involved in multi-level herbals. He was involved in multi-level vitamins. He was involved in multi-level cleansing formulas. ... And so forth.

So, I said to him, "I don't want to be personal and, believe me, I don't want to be presumptuous in any way, but can I just ask you a simple question? How much money do you make a month?" And he said, "Gee, Larry, I feel kind of embarrassed." I said, "I appreciate that and you don't have to answer it, but I'm just curious. How much money do you make a month?" And he said, "Well, last month has been my best month so far." And I said, "So far in terms of what?" He said, "So far, since I quit my job and started my own business!" So, I said, "How long ago was that?" And he said, "About two years ago." I said, "Okay, last month, how much did you make?" He said, "$1,800." I said, "Two years later, you've made $1,800 in one month and during this entire two years, is this the stuff you've been doing?" And he said "yes," but that he's also tried to represent some other products.

So, I said, "You know, my friend, let me make a suggestion to you. You know what you appear to be? . . . A starving man within an oasis of banquets. You've got a feast over yonder waiting for you. And a banquet out there. And, until such time as you stop jumping from one to another, and you commit to the banquet waiting for you, the most you're going to be making is $1,800 a month."

I don't want to be presumptuous or disrespectful in any way, for any number of reasons, not the least of which is that money isn't everything and certainly not for many of us. So, don't take my comments inappropriately. But I will tell you this: if you're dabbling with a little bit of this and a little bit of that, let me make a suggestion. Whatever you're dabbling in, pack it up, stick it in a box, put a tape around it and put it in your garage. Pick a direction – a single direction – you're prepared to commit to, and then commit to it.

The second Attribute of Success is that thing which allows you to go from zero income and zero assets to success as you define it. And that, simply put, requires Single-Mindedness of Purpose.

III. Commitment to Personal Responsibility

The third Attribute of Success goes past Professional Competency and Single-Mindedness of Purpose; number three is what I call a Commitment to Personal Responsibility.

What do I mean by Personal Responsibility? Starting first with what I do not mean is your taking blame for things that other people do or your beating yourself up for things that you do. What I want to suggest is as follows: personal responsibility is the experience you live that you're the cause of everything that happens in your life. Listen to me again. Personal Responsibility is the experience that *you're the cause* of everything that happens in your life.

Think about it for just a second. Everything that has occurred in your life – all of those outcomes – who do you think created them? You're 21 years old. You're 35 years old. You're 45 years old. You're 60 years old. You're 70 years old. Behind you lies a patchwork of events, relationships, wins, losses, joys, and sorrows. Do they belong to someone else? Were they created by someone else? Of course not. They are yours. Own them. You are the only constant for each and every moment in your life, aren't you?

What I want to suggest to you is that unsuccessful behavior is trying to find all of the scapegoats for the results you have, in fact, produced in your life. Successful behavior is embracing, very simply, the notion that if it happened, you did it. Who do you think did? Now, I'm not talking about matters divine. I'm talking about the affairs of mankind. And just know that in our realm, in the realm of human beings, if it happened, you did it. So, own it – all of it.

This is not a theoretical conversation. I'm being very practical with you. I am not talking about philosophy. I am talking about attributes of being successful. And what I am saying is that a cardinal attribute of a successful person is the attribute that says if it happened, I did it. If it's going to happen, I've got to do it. Nobody else. Because you can't rely on anybody else. So, when it comes to Personal Responsibility, let's not worry about the left. Let's not worry about the right. It doesn't matter who lives in your neighborhood, or is a member of your club or church. It doesn't matter who you come across at work. It doesn't matter if they've tried different things to make money and then come to you and say, "Oh! I couldn't make money that way. You'll never make money that way." The fact is there's only one person who can produce a result in your life and that's you.

As much as I want everyone I come across in life and all of my friends to be successful, the fact of the matter is whether they are or are not gives me no permission to be anything other than successful myself. Because, at the end of the day, I am the only one who can ultimately affect outcomes in my life. And when I

SEVEN ATTRIBUTES OF SUCCESS

see it that way, here's what I get out of it. When I don't like an outcome I create, all I have to do is change the behavior and I'll get a different outcome. If I like the outcome, I can replicate the behavior and I'll get a similar outcome. But the only way I can process through that mindset is to realize that I'm the one who created the original outcome to start with.

My suggestion is that you not listen to anyone to your left or to your right. Don't take a look at past outcomes. It doesn't make any difference if the sun is shining or it's not. Or you feel well, or you don't. There's only one person who can create your outcomes and that's going to be you.

The third Attribute of Success – the third attribute that will get you from wherever you are to where you want to be in life – is the attribute I call a Commitment to Personal Responsibility: realizing there's only one person who can produce outcomes in your life and that's you.

IV. Commitment to Effective Conduct

The fourth Attribute of Success is Commitment to Effective Conduct.

What does a Commitment to Effective Conduct look like?

I have always tended to be somewhat amused by motivational speakers. Most (but not all) motivational speakers produce the adrenaline of euphoria, but, at the end of the day, they tend to leave us wanting for specifics. The Fourth Attribute of Success here has very little to do with motivation and a great deal to do with technique.

If you want to make $250,000 a year; if you want to have $1,000,000 at the end of three years: what type of conduct is going to produce that?

It has three parts. It consists of the following:

1. An objective understanding of where you are at the present time (your current reality).
2. A clear understanding of exactly where you want to be (your vision).
3. A specific implementation plan to get you from #1 to #2.

There are three parts, not one, to creating Effective Conduct.

I have listened to any number of motivational speakers over the past forty years and I have read more books than I care to acknowledge. But what I can assure you is that there is no one who can simply will their way into Effective Conduct. I have yet to find a successful individual, irrespective of how you define success, who has simply "willed" their way into wins. *Broadway* is fantastic and the *Music Man* is one of my favorites. But, at the end of the day, will, in itself, does not play a musical instrument. Musical technique – conduct – does, and that's what we are talking about here.

It does take more than "goal setting" to be effective, but it doesn't take more than these three steps. What works? An objective understanding of your current reality, a clear understanding of your vision, and a specific implementation plan to get you from one to the other. That always works, in every context.

Let's discuss each one of those three.

What does "objectively understanding your current reality" look like? Well, think about it for a second. "Objectively" means you don't make it good and you don't make it bad. It just is what it is. So, for example, you have $1,000 in the bank right now. You have $500 in the bank right now. I talk to some people with $500 in the bank and they feel like they've got a million bucks. I talk to other people with $500 in the bank and they feel like they're

SEVEN ATTRIBUTES OF SUCCESS

losers and they have no way out. And, ironically, the common denominator is that they both have $500 in the bank. It's not good. It's not bad. It just is. You've got $500 in the bank. So what? Your attitude did not change that circumstance one bit. You might feel good about it; you might feel badly about it and you know what? You still have $500 in the bank.

The fact is, if you're going to be effective, you have to start off understanding the circumstances under which you will be operating. It's like the military general on the ground. The general goes into a field of battle. Does it matter whether it's good or bad that the troops are amassed across the line? It doesn't make one bit of difference because, you know what? No matter whether it's good or it's bad . . . the simple fact is that it is! And if that general expects to win that battle, he or she better make sure they've done something about those troops that are there. The first aspect of Effective Conduct is being intensely objective in understanding exactly what your circumstances are because, in the final analysis, I don't care if you have ten dollars in the bank. If you have ten dollars in the bank and you have an effective system for producing $10,000, you're going to be making $10,000 in no time at all. But the simple fact is that you have to start with an objective understanding of where you are.

What's number two? It's a clear understanding of your vision – where you want to be. What does "clear" mean from my perspective? You want $10,000 in the bank? You want to make $250,000 a year? That's great! I want you to achieve that also. Now, when do you plan on doing that? At what point can you determine that you are, in fact, heading toward a particular direction?

Nowadays, business language which describes this particular component of Effective Conduct is called OCR's, an acronym for *Objective Critical Results*. In other words, what are we trying to achieve? If I understand where I've come from – where I've started from – and I want to know where I want to be, the question in front of me is how do I know that I am either there or getting there? That requires an enormous clarity with respect to where "there" actually is!

You want $10,000 in the bank and you want it six months from now? I want you to write that down because if you objectively understand where you are, and you very clearly understand where you want to be, now you have an opportunity to get to number three.

What is number three? By Implementation Plan, I mean a *granular and specific* Implementation Plan. The question you are asking is how do you plan on making it happen? What I don't want to hear is, "Larry, I'm going to just go out and do it." That's great, but what are you doing when you're going out and doing it? What I am saying is, what is your specific action plan for getting the job done? How are you solving for your OCRs? Regardless of where you are standing, and regardless of where you want to end up, what's the road map you plan on traversing to connect those two data points.

What I want to see from you is a very specific Implementation Plan which incorporates a timeline and milestones along the way. If you create the Plan, the timeline and the milestones, you now have something to work. Listen, I'm not talking about how you're going to go quit your job. I am not suggesting any particular Plan for you, since I don't know your life circumstances. What I am suggesting, however, is that without one, you have no chance of achieving or at least being intentional at creating results.

It would literally be as if I wanted to go see you, so I got in my car and started driving, not knowing where I'm starting from, where you lived, or how long I have to get there.

Again, this is not theoretical. It's quite real. I have had the good fortune to interact with several hundred thousand people in my career in business: some in the cash flow industry, others in my business law practice, and many others in industries in which I've been involved. In addition, I have spoken to over one million people across the country who are just as motivated as you and the other readers of this book. The simple reality is that the successful ones are the ones who are committed to Effective Conduct. Because – think about it – you will never be able to gain in the totality of your life what you lose in the quality of each individual day. If you allow yourself the opportunity to be effective day to day, you will have given yourself the opportunity to be effective with all of your days.

Effective Conduct: know where you are; know where you want to be; and then move to take steps from one to the other one day at a time.

V. Commitment to Perseverance

Let's discuss the fifth Attribute of Success – what it takes to become successful. I call that the Commitment to Perseverance. What do I mean by Perseverance? What I do not mean is you dredging through the desert on a camel. Fighting snow storms. Relentlessly charging ahead. That's not what I mean. Perseverance can sound pretty daunting, right? That's not what I'm dealing with. When I talk about Perseverance what I mean is *giving yourself the chance to become successful?*

I have come across so many people – intelligent people; well-intentioned people – who, every time they were about ready to break free, to break through, every time they would go off in some other direction. I know a fellow in Orlando, where I'm from. Each time I see this fellow, he's doing something different. I see him in downtown Orlando walking the streets because our offices are in downtown Orlando right there on Orange Avenue, which is sort of the central thoroughfare. I see this fellow in front of our local Starbucks and I say, "Hey Ken, how are you doing?" He says, "Larry, man I'm doing great." He's always doing great. Every time I see him he's doing great. It really annoys me in the morning. And so I say, "Great, Ken, so what are you doing?" He says, "Larry, right now I am representing a printing company. This is the most outrageous printing company you've ever seen. This company does 18-color photography." And I say, "Eighteen colors? Ken, I thought there were only six basic colors out there." He says, "I know. They do 18. I don't even know where the owner found those extra colors. It is the most amazing printing company. Can I come show you their work?" And I say, "Absolutely, my friend. Show me their work. I'd love to see it. You know I do a lot of printing."

Three months later I see him on the street. "Hey Ken, how are you doing?" He says, "Hey Larry, I'm doing great! I'm doing fantastic!" I say, "That's great, Ken. You're always doing very well. So, what are you up to? Printing, right? And he says, "Printing? Nah, forget about that. Larry, can I talk to you about something?" I said, "Sure, Ken." Then he takes a glass out of his pocket. This is in downtown Orlando. It's in the middle of the street and he takes a glass out of his pocket. He says, "Larry, have you ever taken a glass, put it underneath your kitchen sink, put water in the glass, held it up to the light, and looked at the glass? Looked at the water? The grime, the grease and the toxins just polluting your body? Have you ever done that?" And I say, "No, Ken. I can't say that I have." He says, "Larry, I've got a little machine that I can put right underneath your sink so that the next time you decide to drink water, it's going to be as clean as the Colorado River. Can I come show you?" And I say, "Anytime, my friend." Anytime you want to come show me, you show me. Okay, take care of yourself, Ken. Bye."

Three months later I see him on the street. Obviously, he never contacted me, right? And the ritual goes on. "Hey Ken, how are you doing?" And he says, "Larry, let me tell you, if it were any better, I couldn't stand it." And I say, "Water purifiers, right?" And he says, "Water puri... Nah, forget about that. Larry, can I ask you something?" And I say, "Of course, Ken. You always ask me something." He says, "I've got something now. Have you ever heard of this company? It's called … ."

Ken is a real human being and Ken's story is a real story, as exaggerated as it sounds. There have been countless others over the years who, like Ken, in different proportions, simply chased one pursuit after another.

Lately, I have had interaction with an individual who can honestly be described as the smartest guy in the room whenever he is in a meeting. And yet, despite his talents and his skills, he continues to be dazzled by zeros on a financial statement which has him chasing one rainbow after another in pursuit of riches. Is he intelligent? Absolutely. Is he educated? You bet. An absolute pedigree. However, what he lacks is a commitment to perseverance, a critical element of successful conduct.

Sincerely, I don't mean to be disrespectful to Ken, who is a real live human being, and it's a real story. And I don't mean to be disrespectful to the countless others I have come across who exhibit in different proportions, the same type of behavior.

Perseverance, for heaven's sake. How are you ever going to gain momentum driving your car on a city street? You hit stop signs. You have pedestrians. You have red lights, green lights, traffic. If you want to gain momentum in your life, get yourself on a highway, put your foot down on the gas and forget about the exit signs. Otherwise, you end up living your life bouncing off of walls. If that's the doorway, go for the doorway, and for heaven's sake, don't constantly keep your eyes open for new doorways. Otherwise, every single time you hit a resistance point, you're going to go off in a different direction.

Once again, I'm not speaking theoretically with you. We're talking about attributes it takes to become successful. There is not one successful person in this country who became successful in two weeks, or in six weeks, three months, or in six months. The reason they're successful is because they not only had what I called earlier Single-Mindedness of Purpose, which allowed them to focus their attention on one particular thing, but they also had a Commitment to Perseverance – a commitment to see it through to a successful outcome.

Let me make one other suggestion as to why I'm somewhat impassioned with respect to this point on Perseverance. It's because of the fact that I have seen and spoken to so many people across the country in my professional career who did not need to be languishing where they were. Ken, by the way, is a good-looking guy. He's taller than I am, well dressed, he even has several degrees behind his name. There's no reason he, like others, should not be successful. He just hasn't given himself the chance to be successful.

The travesty implied in this kind of conduct, like Ken's – when you're about to seize on something, you go in a different direction – is that pretty soon, it becomes insidious. What I mean by that, is that pretty soon, you begin to believe deep inside your gut that you're not successful as a person. But that's hogwash. It's not that you're not successful as a person. You just haven't given yourself the chance to be successful.

Do you truly want to be successful? Here's my challenge to you. Choose a direction – whatever the direction – based on the research, study, experience, and intuition you have. And then commit to it. If you want to go in a different direction thereafter, you will have to earn your way out. How do you earn your way out? By being successful at what you do. You see, if you're successful at what you do and you decide to make an affirmative choice to do something else, then you will be successful at that too. Do you know why? Because you're going to take into that next thing – whatever it might be – an attitude of being successful because you were successful in that first choice.

So here is my challenge to you. It kind of sounds like *The Firm*, the movie. Make a choice. Pick a direction. And pursue it with single-mindedness of purpose and commitment. Do whatever you want to do, but you may not change your mind and you may not take an exit ramp off that highway unless and until you have earned the right by being successful. Commit to Perseverance.

VI.   Commitment to Integrity

The sixth Attribute of Success is a Commitment to Integrity. It is the human manifestation of Absolute Truth. It's called Integrity. Truth in the absolute is a perfect representation of itself. Integrity on the human level is abiding and living as closely as we can to that highest truth. And what I'm saying to you, as much as what we see around us, is that you can't be successful without integrity.

I know you read that and you said, "Larry that flies in the face of my experience." But I say to you, no it doesn't. Not really. You come across people once in a while who are, in fact, multi-millionaires or even billionaires, but I will tell you that it rarely lasts. I remember talking to my father several years ago about a big scandal in Orlando with one of our Central Florida movers and shakers. He and a bunch of people were indicted, a story covered on the front page of the *Orlando Sentinel*. And Dad, modest as he always was as a man, turned to me, and he said, "You know what, Larry? Even the mighty, so shall they fall. It's only a question of time."

The fact is, it doesn't do anyone any good and it won't do you any good to focus 100% on money alone if, in the meantime, you end up losing your soul. I don't mean that, by the way, in a religious sense, and I'm not using this chapter to expound religious doctrine to you. I'm saying it in a very human sense. I'm saying we are business people second. We are human beings first. And if we allow ourselves to commit to acting in the highest level of integrity with everything we do, then, we may make mistakes! I make mistakes all the time. Mistakes are inevitable for each of us. But when we make those mistakes, we don't make them because our commitment isn't there. We make them because we made the wrong decision. We didn't happen to get it right this time.

And I also want to make another suggestion to you. I take my mission very seriously and my mission is to seek out the truth, to find it, and to communicate it to the best of my ability. My intention is to influence you not only to be successful in business, but also as a human being. My objective is to influence you to become a better person tomorrow than you are today – a commitment I have made to myself which is part of my daily mantra.

Attribute number six – A Commitment to Integrity.

VII. Commitment to Love and Caring: Other Serving

The seventh and final Attribute of Success you are going to read and then say to yourself that I have fallen off the grid, is the human manifestation of the Absolute Principle. What's the Absolute Principle? Love.

Seriously, Larry?

How do I mean that in real-life terms? How about just simple caring? Just simple caring.

There are only two ways in which you can operate in life and there are only two ways in which you can operate in business. Number one is by what I call "being Self Serving." The other is what I call "being Other Serving." Self-Serving or Other Serving! That's it. You only have two choices because you can't truly serve two masters. You are either going to serve yourself or you're going to serve somebody else.

I want to suggest to you is that if you are Self Serving as a person, what you do once successful is that you take these attributes and you end up serving yourself. If you are Self Serving, you take all of this information at your disposal – and your knowledge and your skills and your competencies – and you use those things to serve yourself and even manipulate circumstances if necessary.

What does somebody who is Other Serving do? Do they have skills? Do they have competencies? Yes, they do. They have those skills and those competencies, but what they do is they use them to benefit other people. Is there an opportunity to profit then from that? Of course there is. Because they've invested in acquiring their skills. They've invested themselves in their competencies and they deserve to be rewarded for that.

So, what's the difference? The difference is in the perspective in the value-for-value exchange. It provides you value in exchange for whatever the fair price is that others are prepared to pay me for that value. That's an exchange which underlies every business – and even human – transaction. But never, never, never confuse business with being Self Serving, because it just doesn't have to be. Business is a value exchange. Who you serve is your perspective.

You see, the fact is that I'm not talking about making a profit. I'm talking about the motivation under, and by which, you make a profit. And I'm suggesting to you that if you want to become and remain successful, the attribute supporting that effort is caring for others—being Other Serving.

I am gently making these two last points. And, in doing so, I want to make sure you recognize that I do not operate in that way all of the time. In fact, I am not proselytizing or suggesting that it is even possible, because life does have a tendency to invalidate the best of our intentions. That notwithstanding, I am suggesting that these are where your intentions should lie, and from those intentions, your commitments. After all, think about it for just a minute. If you are operating on a day-by-day basis committed to the highest level of integrity and the highest level of caring for others, how in the world can you possibly go wrong? Yes, you will make mistakes, but they will be mistakes of application, not of intention. But your intentions nonetheless will be there supporting your growth towards successful and effective living.

SUMMARY

We have covered a lot of material in what is otherwise a relatively short chapter in this book.

Let me use the final opportunity to summarize the *Seven Attributes of Success* from my experience.

1. **Commitment to Professional Competency**. What is it? It is knowing your business like the back of your hand.

2. **Commitment to Single-Mindedness of Purpose**. What is it? Making sure you are focused and on purpose in everything you do.

3. **Commitment to Personal Responsibility**. What is it? It is experiencing yourself as the cause, not the effect, of everything that happens in your life.

4. **Commitment to Effective Conduct**. What is it? It is understanding your current reality, understanding your vision, and charting a clear path to get from one to the other.

5. **Commitment to Perseverance**. What is it? It is giving yourself the chance to become successful by refusing to take an exit ramp from the highway until you have become successful on the highway you are driving.

6. **Commitment to Integrity**. What is it? It is living consistently with your highest truth.

7. **Commitment to Caring**. What is it? It is being rewarded for the value you bring by being fully committed to others.

I hope my perspectives were valuable to you. All my best and God bless in your endeavors!

About Larry

Laurence J. (Larry) Pino, Esq. is the Founder and CEO of Tuscan Gardens. Prior to founding the company in 2010, he was the Founder and CEO of Dynetech®, a private equity development and management company focused on starting, developing and growing business enterprises. He has served as Chairman or Board Member for many of those investments. He has created some 80 businesses in his professional career selling over $1.5 billion of goods and services, employing several thousand employees and generating half a billion dollars of investment capital. Over the past 35 years, Mr. Pino has transacted numerous real estate, stock, and investment ventures for himself and his clients exceeding $1 billion in value.

By background, Larry is a commercial litigation attorney specializing in business and investment law. He graduated with a Bachelor's Degree from the University of Notre Dame and a J.D. degree from New York University Law School. He has received Certificates of Study from the University of Madrid, L'Alliance Francaise in Paris, and the Centro Linguistico Italiano Dante Alighieri in Rome. Subsequently, he was admitted to practice law and is in good standing as a member of the bars in Florida, New York, and California, as well as in various federal courts across the country.

In the last 30 years, Larry has conducted some 5,500 speaking engagements, speaking to over one million people and appearing on 140 radio and television talk shows. He currently teaches a course on *Rapid Enterprise Development* for the Hamilton Holt School at Rollins College in Winter Park, Florida, as an Adjunct Professor, and he is pursuing a Doctorate in Business Administration at the Warrington College of Business at the University of Florida.

Larry has authored nine books including among others: *Finding Your Niche* (Berkley-Putnam Publishing), *Finding Your E-Niche, The Desktop Lawyer,* and *Cash In On Cash Flow* (Simon & Schuster). He also co-authored *Morphing: Radical Evolution for Revolutionary Times* with Dr. Craig McAllaster, retired Acting President Emeritus of Rollins College.

Larry is married with three sweethearts (two boys and a girl), who are the center of his life.

CHAPTER 3

CHANGING THE CONVERSATION

BY CHAMBRIA J. HENDERSON

Years ago, I was leading a team of volunteers at a weekend event that featured former President Ronald Reagan and Zig Ziglar as guest speakers. The long hours and physical labor was tough duty but the dividends were huge. Saturday night, after the crowds had cleared the coliseum and most of the volunteers had gone back to their rooms, the leaders of each volunteer team were called backstage.

I was ushered behind closed curtains to stage left where Mr. Ziglar was sitting on one of the props casually speaking with the other 8-10 volunteer leaders. He told us he enjoyed staying after events to speak to the volunteers because he saw in us people who were willing to do whatever it takes to make a difference, people who lived their lives for the greater good and with passion, and he was energized by our attitudes.

He asked each of us in turn why we had volunteered and what we were passionate about. He listened intently, asked specific questions and gave encouragement. The setting was so intimate that when he spoke to us specifically, we felt as if we were the only person in the room and yet, we were privileged to eavesdrop on every conversation.

When he addressed me, I confessed I volunteered because I couldn't afford the event ticket but the line-up of speakers was manna to my soul. Having to work hard and dirty and invisible for that privilege was irrelevant. When he asked about my passion, I told him I was born to make a difference behind the scenes as a work-horse that would allow strong leaders to emerge powerfully with their visions of a better community. From an early age, I had a knack and track record for connecting people to causes bigger than themselves. Personally, I knew I wanted to affect K-12 education and felt my then-current job of being a fundraiser in the political arena was foundational to developing a rapport of trust with decision-makers.

When I finished speaking, Mr. Zigler spoke with gravity, "Promise me. Say it out loud. Promise yourself. Promise those you have and haven't met yet who need your talents and passion to get themselves to the next level. Promise the children who haven't been born yet, that you will do something every day of your life that will bring about a better education for them than what is available today." He didn't let me just nod my head in agreement. He didn't move on until I had passionately voiced an unbreakable vow that I would do whatever it took, no matter the cost, and without excuses, to further the work of bringing educational excellence to America's children. It was a promise I've kept.

Now, to back up just a bit, lest anyone think I'm sanguine by nature and enjoy hobnobbing among the rich and powerful for the sake of the poor and powerless. Let me assure you, getting beyond my own social awkwardness was the demon I had to confront daily. I can't count the number of times, in the early years, when I purposely showed up late to meetings hoping to walk in unnoticed, or worse, just turned around and went home without ever going inside, or how many times I fled networking events or how many podiums I walked away from, because I was shaking so hard I couldn't see my notes or remember my speech, or how many times I passed out due to fear.

Forcing myself to tame the beast within, relentlessly demanding my silence, became my over-riding goal. *"Whatever it takes, no matter the cost, without excuse. . ."* became my mantra. Slowly, painfully, I began to realize the message was more important than remaining invisible and cowering to my fears. I recognized I was cheating the masses out of a new and different future. I was playing too small to make a big difference. I knew if I were to make a difference that would be felt for generations I had to "speak in spite of my voice shaking."

Although being a political fundraiser challenged me to my core, as I warmed up to it, it became a great game to play. Every candidate needed money to run their campaign. Their campaigns lived, died, or thrived based on their fundraising skills. The newbies usually had breath-taking passion and promises but felt uncomfortable asking for money. They needed someone with expertise to work and grow their small circles of influence. On the other end of the spectrum, the seasoned politicians needed experienced workhorses and new energy on their teams to get re-elected. They appreciated being able to show up at events and rally the troops without having to do all of the event planning and fundraising legwork on their own.

Business was good, but more important than the money and the resume was the personal contacts I was making. Having worked on campaigns for almost every office, from precinct committeeman and school boards to city, state, congressional, and presidential campaigns, the contacts were my ultimate capital. I respected and valued every relationship, whether or not I agreed with the ideology. Every contact opened new doors and new possibilities either for me or for someone I worked with. Finding common ground on both sides of the aisle opened opportunities that had previously seemed to be riddled with impenetrable roadblocks. I learned to genuinely listen without prejudice, judgement, or opinion for the sake of the greater good.

One day, one of my candidates asked what I would do if I could affect any area of public policy. My response was immediate, "Create a tax credit that would allow any child in Arizona to attend the school of their parents' choosing." He said it was an idea whose time had come and asked what I had done toward making it a reality. I told him that although I was a political fundraiser, I didn't know enough about the political process, per se, to have done anything about it. He told me that if he lost his election (which he did), he would work tirelessly with me to bring my vision to fruition through the legislative process.

That simple conversation led to a three-year legislative battle to introduce a concept that was the first of its kind in the Nation. From the Arizona legislature to the U.S. Supreme Court, the law made its way through the system by the narrowest of margins. Today, twenty years later, some form of that original concept is ensconced in the law books of **seventeen states** and directly affects the lives of hundreds of thousands of federal poverty and state working poor K-12 students and their families annually.

Watching the vision that started at my kitchen table, spreading across the Nation giving families a hope in their future and a way out of the poverty they have known for generations is humbling, exciting, gut-wrenching and inspiring.

I read thousands of letters every year from members of the community and grateful parents whose children are getting a personalized education they could never afford otherwise. The education mirrors the values being taught in the home and encompasses the three "R's" plus character development, life skills, and community involvement. Students are pro-actively being taught to seek out and give back the best life has to offer.

Now, after having raised almost $60M and awarding tuition assistance to over 20,000 K-12 students in Arizona, the final phase of my vision is calling to me. It's time to move forward once again. This time, however, I will be taking the first step in being the change I want to see happen and hoping others will follow my lead.

My journey over the past twenty plus years has shown people are passionate about education. Some have only opinions to offer. Others, the real champions in the education arena, have hands-on time, expertise, and/or financial assistance to offer. The moms and dads, extended families, teachers, coaches, community members, innovators, local organizations, and businesses, all with skin in the game and willing to give of their time, talents, and resources, are the real deal. They are the ones on whose shoulders our children will stand. It's time to begin pro-actively shifting the national education conversation away from the negativity that abounds and begin engaging the pace-setters and innovators who have a track record of successful, specific, measurable results. It's time to showcase what is working in our K-12 public and private schools and calling on our decision-makers to take action accordingly.

But here's the problem and a partial solution: The 1983 report, *A Nation at Risk*, succinctly summarized major problems within the American public education system. The report, right or wrong, was seen as a clarion call-to-action and spurred reform efforts on all levels. During the past 35 years, we have seen numerous innovations in the K-12 education arena and extraordinary opposition to all of it. Each follow-up report shows the same thing; not enough has been done in some areas and too much has been done in other areas. At every turn, we hear how awful and burdensome our education system is and how it is failing our children and how American students don't measure up to their global peers AND we hear how horrible and damaging every new idea is or will be that has been presented, that could or has changed the system.

Because many of the new ideas are considered "disruptive innovations," both the opposition and the support of them are intense and ongoing. Those who wish to maintain the status quo in K-12 education fiercely oppose the innovations and accompanying body of laws surrounding them while those who wish to encourage innovation are pushing forward with dogged determination. The tipping point hasn't occurred yet, but the push and pull toward it is gaining momentum.

The problems are real and need to be addressed; however, when the national conversation focuses on only the problems, there isn't room for solutions. The negativity distracts from and then over-powers and silences any common-ground solutions that may be presented. In the meantime, our children continue to grow up, moving through a broken system that seems, at best, to have stalled out when it comes to real reform, and at its worst, leaves us with more of what we already have that we don't like.

Yet, in both our K-12 public and private schools (and their many variations), we have pockets of success across the Nation where positive change is occurring among our most vulnerable children. In some schools, we see our poor and minority children graduating from high school and going on to college at a higher rate than their neighboring schools. In other areas, we see our elementary students' math and reading skills improve by double digits over their similar peer groups. Across the county we hear of principals, teachers, community leaders, and even celebrities taking a personal interest in the students they have a heart for, and having a profound impact on their lives. These pockets of success are the seeds of change.

We have all heard the mantra "change your words, change your world." The next phase of systemic change requires a shifting of our national conversation away from what won't or isn't working toward what is working and then building upon it.

Currently, our Extra Credit Show podcasts are exploring educational innovations with the innovators themselves. We're seeking to discover the foundations and driving forces behind the innovations and exploring the implementation and evolution of their ideas. We're seeking to understand issues surrounding their work and challenging methods of accountability. We're also sharing the stories that have been lost to the masses; stories of defeat and devastation that have ultimately turned to triumph for our children. We believe if we are authentically listening and searching for common ground, we will change the national conversation, resulting in being able to build a future together that empowers our children. We will do whatever it takes . . . no matter the cost, and without excuse.

About ChamBria

ChamBria J. Henderson is passionate about making a difference in other peoples' lives. From her earliest days of being "the big sister" in a large multi-racial, USAF family that was always filled with foster kids, to her first neighborhood fundraiser at the age of 9, she has always looked out for the lost and lonely and under-privileged in society. She loves few things more than listening to others until they get done talking, and encouraging them to find their best self and chase their dreams.

Being a military brat, she experienced first-hand the disparity in education in classrooms across the United States. Often attending several schools in a year, she found herself either at the top or bottom of the new class on a regular basis. Frustrated with one of her 5th grade teachers, she demanded and was appalled to learn from the principal that school choice was not a legal option. She informed him that someday it would be. The upside to that situation was that she learned the power of, and has enjoyed self-educating since then, always competing against herself to master the unknown. Graduating in the top 3% of her high school class and still feeling unprepared for the adult world, she realized systemic change in K-12 education needed to happen and she wanted to be a part of the transition.

Through the years, ChamBria has been fortunate to connect with the founders and leaders in the education reform and school choice movements. She has also connected with strong leaders and innovators in our traditional education system. She finds value in every educational setting and believes that whatever the setting, education is the key to our success as a nation, a community, and as individuals.

The Extra Credit Show is not a show espousing a particular ideology or opinion. Instead, in her podcasts, ChamBria is reaching out to those who are making a difference in our children's lives. She is interviewing people from all walks of life, who have impacted education, with a track record of successful and meaningful results. She is bringing authentic, active listening into the American conversation about education and what is best for our children.

For more information, you can connect with her at:
- chambria@gmail.com
- chambriahenderson.com

CHAPTER 4

FINDING TRUE NORTH: BUILDING THE LIFE YOU WANT

BY MARY ANN KEHLER

It was after dark when I got home that night. It had been a long and grueling day – starting with a three-hour flight the night before, followed by a full day of teaching and meetings, and ending with the flight home and the drive from the airport. I opened the front door, put my briefcase in its usual spot … and suddenly didn't want to be there. I was tired. I was grumpy. I wanted out of those four walls. More importantly, I wanted out of my life.

But then, something amazing happened. I stopped thinking about how my 5'5" frame now weighed 204 pounds, about how it had been forever since I'd gotten any real exercise. I stopped thinking about how I would cringe every time I looked in the mirror, about how frustrating it was to keep "outgrowing" all my clothes.

I started thinking about the story I had read on the plane the night before. Lisa Allen's story, which I'd found in Charles Duhigg's book, *The Power of Habit*. I thought about how Lisa's life had turned around the day she decided she wanted to go on a trek through the Egyptian desert. How that decision had led her to decide to quit smoking, because she knew she'd need stamina. How that decision had eventually led to yet another ... and then another, and another. How, four years later, she'd gotten over her divorce, lost 60 pounds, run a marathon, started a master's degree, resolved her credit problems, and bought a home.

I noticed that the night was starlit and particularly beautiful, that the temperature was a comfortable 70 degrees. Inspired by Lisa's story, I changed into an old pair of sneakers, grabbed my keys and phone, and headed out the front door. Thirty minutes and one mile later, I walked back in through the front door. But this time was different. This time, I felt refreshed and ... happy. The next night, I remembered that feeling, and I remembered Lisa. I didn't hesitate. Sneakers. Keys. Phone. And out the door ... for a bit longer this time. By the third night, I was hooked. I simply couldn't wait to get home, just so that I could start my walk.

When I awoke on the fourth morning, I started wondering what would happen if I cut back on carbs. Maybe only one serving per day? A week later, I'd lost three pounds. After a month, I'd lost ten pounds, my clothes were comfortably loose, and sleep was coming more easily. The sneakers wore out; I bought walking shoes. I began to wonder what would happen if I cut back on refined sugar. Could I reduce my intake by half? That one was tough – I've always loved sweets. But I'd become hooked on the idea of feeling better, so I stuck with it. The walks gradually increased to three miles a day, and the pounds slowly disappeared. At the minus-30 mark, friends began commenting on how great I looked. I bought hiking boots and smaller clothing. I was excited about being more active.

Then my right knee was injured and my physical therapist put me on a stationary bike for recovery. I joined a gym, and discovered that working out could actually be **fun**. I'm now at the gym four times a week. On the non-gym days, I'm out the door in my walking shoes for the three miles that have become my time for mental clearing. I've lost 50 pounds. I've discovered Yoga. Most importantly, I feel terrific. I'm already planning my celebration – I'm going to hike the trails on the coast of Scotland in 2018.

How did all this happen? By developing good habits. The habit of changing into sneakers for the nightly walk. The habit of eating carbs only once a day. The habit of avoiding sugar and dairy. The habit of hitting the gym four times a week, even when my schedule is jammed.

What does all that have to do with my business? A great deal, as it turns out.

I'm a vocal coach, a voice teacher, a teacher trainer. My students are professional performers and aspiring professionals, including a significant number of high school students who plan to study performing arts in college. My job is to help them identify – and then get – what they want. For the professionals, it's a hit song or a theatre role or a steady job doing what they love. For high school students, it's the college program of their dreams. For teachers, it's building a business that fits their lives and their goals.

Several years ago, I started working with Colin, the lead singer of a local rock band. He asked me for help with some vocal problems. Colin's a good musician, but the band wasn't taking off the way that he wanted – they weren't getting enough gigs to build a following, or to make any real money. Even when they did get gigs, they would sometimes have to cancel because Colin's voice failed.

Colin had a day job, but always seemed to have financial shortages. He couldn't scrape together enough money to buy a $40 steamer that would have helped with his vocal problems. He would frequently cancel our sessions, saying that he just didn't have the funds. Eventually, he stopped making appointments altogether.

There are a lot of musicians who, like Colin, just can't seem to "make it big." Talented songwriters whose work has never been published. Gifted performers who are still, at age 30, playing for tips in neighborhood coffee shops while dreaming of a bigger stage. Musical theatre graduates with no idea how to begin building their career – because they chose a college that didn't meet their needs, because they never examined their strengths and weaknesses or thought about what they wanted their lives to be like.

I started to wonder how I could help them succeed.

The answer came during my interview with Caroline, a prospective student. Seemingly out of nowhere, I asked her: "What do you see yourself doing in 10 years?" She looked surprised: "Performing on Broadway." The light bulb went on. Then I asked her, "What do you see yourself doing in 20 years?" She responded, "That's a long time from now, but I'd say still performing and perhaps directing." Finally, I asked her, "What do you want from a college program?" She replied, "To be prepared to audition for professional theatre." Hmmmmm. At 17, she had more clarity than many of the 30-year-olds on my schedule. (Nine years later, Caroline is now performing a lead role on a national tour.)

At first, I couldn't believe it could be that simple. But, after reading stacks of books on success, after observing students who were successful performers, I became convinced – the people who were consistently achieving success knew what they wanted and had a plan to get there. That insight led me to develop a series of questions that can help anyone work toward their life goals. *What do you want? How are you going to get it?* The most important planning you'll ever do begins with envisioning your future.

PART I – WHAT DO YOU WANT?

1. What do you see yourself doing in 10 years?
Time means different things at different stages in our lives. A

60-year-old doctor, a 50-year-old entrepreneur, a 40-year-old thinking about launching a second career, and a 30-year-old performer will all have different views as to how much time they have to work with. Pick the time span that makes sense for you. Your number may be five years, or even two.

Don't turn this into a "to do" list, and don't rush to find the "right" or "expected" answer. Take your time, think about what **you** want your **entire** life to look like.

Do be specific. It's the specifics that inspire us to take action – often, by helping us identify the steps that will lead us "there."

• What will your career look like?
• Do you see yourself following your current path, staying in the same field? Or would you be moving in a different direction? What would that look like?
• Where will you live?
• What kind of house/apartment/condo/loft? What will the furnishings be like?
• Will you be living with others? If so, who?
• How will you spend your free time?

 # 2. What do you see yourself doing in 20 years (or 10, or 5)? Again, use the number that fits your circumstances. Look about twice as far out as you did in question #1.

• What will your career look like? Will your focus have shifted toward another field, or perhaps retirement? Does your current path lead you toward or away from that goal?
• Where will you live? Have you been longing to spend some time living somewhere very different … perhaps Europe or Costa Rica or a South Pacific island? How can you make that happen?
• Is a life partner part of that picture? Children? A dog?

3. What are your 'Top 5'? – the things you enjoy most, the things that make you happy.

What do you love about your life? What is missing? There's nothing too big or too small; remind yourself of what makes you happy, so you can shape your life around it. To get you started, here are my Top 5:

> **Teaching/speaking/performing/directing.** *I am equally happy doing any of the four.*
>
> **Daylight.** *I need lots of it. This is a requirement for my workspace.*
>
> **Good paper.** *I am a paper junkie. Looking at it. Writing on it. Making things from it. I need an hour a week to play with paper or I'm just not happy.*
>
> **Travel.** *If you happen to see me hurrying through an airport with a suitcase in tow, chances are that there is a smile on my face ... even at 2 a.m.*
>
> **Writing.** *I wrote a play at the age of 8. My sibs and I performed it with our friends, for our parents. I was hooked.*

PART II – DO YOU HAVE THE HABITS THAT WILL GET YOU WHAT YOU WANT?

We all have habits. Serious musicians already have the "practice habit" down pat. But it's usually their other habits – seemingly unrelated to music – that end up determining whether they find the success they are seeking. Are your habits helping you on your path – or hampering your efforts? If the latter is true, is it time to make a decision to take control of what is important to you? To revise the habits that aren't leading you toward what you want?

Take control of your time. There was a point during my weight loss saga when I realized that I'd traded one habit for another. I like working out late at night and, as the workouts lengthened, realized I hadn't turned the TV on in six months. And I didn't miss it ... at all.

Take control of your money. I reached out to Colin, the rock singer, and we had a frank talk about his finances. It turned out that he loved shopping at costly department stores, and would max his credit cards to buy designer clothing. Myself, I prefer outlet malls; I gave him a list of my favorites. Now, when he indulges his shopping habit, he doesn't break the bank. More importantly, taking that first step made a huge impact on his career. His voice sounds great now – and the band is getting more gigs. He feels in control of his life. His next step will be to meet with a financial advisor, to map a long-term financial plan for himself and the band.

Take control of your health. Part of my work comes from physician referrals; I help singers rehabilitate their voices after damage or medical problems have required extended vocal rest or surgery (or both). Enter Alicia, who was recovering from surgery to remove a large node from a vocal cord. (In medical circles, we would say "... remove a large nodule from a vocal fold.") Node surgery requires several weeks – at least – of vocal rest. That translates to no talking and no singing – and, for a professional, no work. One of the causes of Alicia's node was that her vocal cords were constantly being irritated by gastrointestinal reflux – caused, in turn, by Alicia's coffee habit. Alicia loved coffee. Couldn't give it up. Months after her voice should have healed, the reflux was growing worse. We had the meeting that every teacher dreads – the one where I had to tell Alicia there was nothing more I could do to help her. Her coffee habit was killing her career. I asked, "Do you want coffee, or do you want a career?" We parted. An hour later, this message rolled into my phone: "I want a career." The change turned out to be so simple: all she really wanted was a hot beverage in her cup. Once she found one that didn't involve coffee, her voice healed, and she was back at work within just a few weeks.

Of course, not every health issue can be solved by something as simple as cutting out coffee. The important thing is to give yourself permission to take care of yourself – and to modify your goals as necessary to find what works for you and your circumstances.

TAKING ACTION – STAY FOCUSED

There are so many ways – from low-tech to high-tech – that will help you stay on track. I keep a document on my laptop titled, *Building The Life I Want*. On the first day of every month, my phone reminds me to review – and update – that document. My monthly "date with the doc" is a reminder that each decision – how I spend my time, manage my money, maintain a healthy lifestyle – affects my overall direction.

In a sense, a habit is nothing more than a recurring decision. When done purposefully, each subsequent decision reinforces the previous ones. Each decision that follows becomes easier. And more quickly than seems possible, those decisions have led to a new habit. It really is as simple as "I'm off to the gym." versus "I'm too tired to work out." So, make it a point, whenever faced with a decision, to ask yourself which option is going to help you get "there", moving you toward the life you want.

Don't be surprised if what you want changes along the way. That's okay. The key is to keep the big picture in plain sight. Keep making conscious decisions and you'll stay on the path to your own "true north."

Reference:
Charles Duhigg, *The Power of Habit: Why We Do What We Do In Life and Business* (New York: Random House, 2012).

About Mary Ann

Mary Ann Kehler has had four distinct careers, spanning over 40 years. Beginning as an office administrator, she quickly discovered a talent for technical writing. That led to a move into computer systems analysis and programming, and establishing a successful business. At 32, she decided to stop ignoring her desire to study music, sold the business, and went back to school. By the time she turned 35, she was directing musicals.

Fifteen years and 65 shows later, Mary Ann decided to focus her work on the individual voice. She became certified as a voice instructor and has since taught more than 42,000 voice lessons. She has become known for her work in rehabilitating damaged voices, and for educating singers to prevent vocal damage. She trains professional performing artists; her work also includes college audition coaching for high school students who want to study theatre and music at the collegiate level.

Along the way, Mary Ann discovered a capacity for helping students define and accomplish their professional and personal goals – even if that led them in directions that had nothing to do with music.

Mary Ann is a founding board member, former Director of Education, and current President of International Voice Teachers of Mix, a non-profit that provides education for voice teachers world-wide. She is also co-founder and Executive Producer of Broadway Training Intensive, a training resource for teens and young adults. She is co-author of the recently published, *College Musical Theatre and Acting Programs: Get Accepted!*

Mary Ann enjoys traveling the world, teaching, writing, and speaking. To learn more about Mary Ann and how she can help you achieve your professional and personal goals, whatever your field, find her at:
- MaryAnnKehler.com
- @MaryAnnKehler (on social media)

CHAPTER 5

HOW TO CREATE AND LAUNCH YOUR OWN ONLINE COURSE

BY GREG ROLLETT

The stage had been set for over a week now. The promotional emails had been written, edited and finally sent out. The registration page was working, steadily collecting names and emails for days.

I decided to pre-record the sales webinar so I could be live on the call, looking at any technical glitches and answering questions in real time without any issues taking me off-path while presenting.

The slide deck and the copy were formatted with 30 minutes of groundbreaking content – followed by what I considered to be a very great offer presentation for a brand-new product I was launching after years of "thinking about it."

It was finally 7pm. The presentation began. Then the 30-minute mark hit. My heart stopped. Would they bite on the offer? Would they click out as soon as I mentioned the price? Would anyone buy?

The moment was so built up in my head that I was an emotional rollercoaster. My browser was open with tabs for Gmail to immediately see when orders came in. PayPal was open to ensure the correct payments would come in and a third window was open for the webinar screen, so I would know if my entire year's worth of work would finally pay off.

The next 20-30 minutes were a blur. My inbox was full of new orders. PayPal was collecting payments and people were redirected to my new product, The New Music Economy. It was my first big win as an online product creator.

Selling Is Like Walking... You Have To Do It Before You Run.

One of the biggest lessons I have learned in business is that no matter what you do, you cannot create income without first selling something. Even in finding a job, you are selling yourself to be paid a specific wage. Then once you have the job, you are selling your time to the company for said wage.

As an entrepreneur or a small business owner, you are always selling. And the sales of your products and services create the lifeblood of your business, cash flow.

The problem is that most new entrepreneurs struggle with getting their product to market. They have hundreds of ideas, they know that they want to change the world and they even know what they are going to do with their future fortunes. We've all been there – constantly daydreaming and staring at our email inboxes wondering why no money is flying out of it like a shiny, silver ATM machine. Didn't my bank account just hear my million-dollar idea?

We have all had our version of the million-dollar idea, but when it comes time to put pen to paper and start, many stop. ...Or at least get stuck.

The Informational Product Mindset

Before I created my first online course, The New Music Economy, I had toiled with hundreds of ideas in my head. … some brilliant. … some made for the garbage bin. … and some not even worthy of the recycling bin (metaphorically speaking).

The discoveries I made during my transition from cubicle dwelling marketing director to online entrepreneur were nothing short of 'eye-opening' and extremely exciting. For starters, the market for selling information is as vast as the oceans – from free reports to cheap eBooks to extensive and expensive research papers, to full-blown multi-media courses. Forbes.com estimates that it was poised to be a 107-billion-dollar industry in 2016 alone.

Online courses and educational programs can range in price from $1 to $10,000. But there was one thing that stood out more than a purple, polka-dotted elephant, … the margins!

My high school math skills were suddenly playing tricks on me. I could create a few videos that helped my marketplace reach a desired outcome; ones that cost me nothing but time, and I could charge $50 each, and never have to ship anything, print anything, or incur overhead of any kind (other than a few cents on my merchant account).

It was music to my ears, literally. … But I was still riddled with doubt.

Overcoming Your Fears In Developing Info Products

During the planning and development of the New Music Economy, I toiled with many of the same fears, doubts and questions that many of you are facing when trying to develop something for the world not only to see, but to purchase, consume and ultimately produce results from. Questions like:

1. How much work am I really getting myself into?
2. Do I really have something to teach that people will pay money for?
3. How do I put it all together?
4. How much should I charge?
5. Do I need case studies and testimonials?
6. How does all the technology work?
7. And so on and so forth…

To get over these fears, I decided to dive headfirst into my market. I wanted to know who the players were. What were they selling? How much were they selling? Were there reviews? Could I buy copies to see their material first hand? What was available in stores and mainstream outlets? Who was paying for keywords in Google and Yahoo? What were the popular Facebook pages and what were they advertising on Facebook and YouTube?

Once you do this for your market, you instantly start to see what is working and what people are demanding.

You also begin your own internal thinking to see what is missing from the market.

In my case, I noticed that most people in the music business and the music marketing niche were focused on either helping musicians get recording contracts, or giving them an intro to social media and social networking, with courses on developing Myspace pages (this was a few years ago when Myspace was cool), Twitter accounts (a new tool just coming onto the market), and the like.

So, based on my experience, I saw a huge gap that I could tap into and create my own lane via my own online course. The product I would later create was a multimedia course teaching musicians how to leverage Internet Marketing and Direct

Marketing strategies to build their fan base and create their own business, so they didn't need to rely on a record label or fancy social networking tools.

I would never have known this had I not understood my industry. Once I learned a significant amount about my industry, as you must do, my fears were put to rest almost immediately. I could now spend my time getting to work and creating my products that would add real value for the people that purchased them.

Building A Winning Product Framework

Getting started is always the hardest part of the process, right? Just like writing this book chapter. The first 20 words are the toughest to write down.

Building your first online course, creating the first video or writing the first words in an eBook are the hardest to move from your mind to consumable media. But before we get to that first step, we can set ourselves up to succeed by planning out our product path and development.

I like to use giant whiteboards, and create the largest brainstorming session I can. You may like traditional outlines using a notebook or Word document. No matter your tool of choice, your goal is to build a framework of what your product will look like.

- Will there be 4 modules? 8? 10? 12?
- What is the process you want to take your customers through?
- What is their ultimate goal?
- What are the main problems that you can solve?
- What can you think of that people will pay for?

What you are looking to create is what I like to call a framework. Wikipedia refers to a conceptual framework with the following definition: *"A **conceptual framework** is used in research to* *outline possible courses of action or to present a preferred approach to an idea or thought."*

To give you further insight into a framework, take the work of some other successful authors and product creators. Stephen Covey wrote his famous book, *The 7 Habits Of Highly Effective People* to highlight the "7 Habits." Those "7 Habits" are the framework for not only his book, but his consulting practice and his high-level training.

Tim Ferriss has now written two best sellers that take on a slightly different framework. In the *The 4-Hour Body* and *The 4-Hour Workweek*, Tim uses the 4-hour framework to teach his readers how to live a better life. In *The 4-Hour Body*, he uses short bursts of body 'hacks' to live healthier, lose weight and gain muscle, which are the results he wishes for his readers to obtain. In *The 4 Hour Workweek*, Tim uses the same quick techniques to effectively manage our time, because getting more time to do the things we care about is the result of the problem most people face – not enough time.

In legendary marketer Frank Kern's *Mass Control* home study course, his framework is based on *30 Days to Mass Control Millions*. His framework takes the customer through four weeks of videos and workbooks to achieve their desired results, which is to build their Internet Marketing business.

In my New Music Economy course, the framework I created is a 4-week video course designed to help musicians become more entrepreneurial through learning direct marketing strategies.

Taking these examples and compiling your own product framework will give you the perfect starting place in getting your product together and to start winning in your marketplace.

Constructing Your Product

Once you have your framework, you now have a blueprint to

guide your customers through to achieve their desired result.

For example, if you want to create a product to help someone lose weight, what is their optimal goal? To lose 50 pounds? If this is the case, your product should help them get to that goal through the course of your product. I'll use a simple 4-module system to illustrate the point.

1. Your first module may be on grocery shopping and changing their mindset towards food.

2. The second module may be to lose that first pound by walking around the block.

3. Your third module builds upon this and helps them get to maybe 20-30 pounds of weight loss through exercise routines, strict meal choices and getting consistent rest.

4. The final module should be your advanced strategies for losing those last 5-10 pounds and give a plan to continue getting into optimal fitness shape. If your product can deliver these four sequences of information, you are providing real value to your marketplace and actually helping people achieve their desired results.

This potent combination will reward you financially as well as internally. Your product has changed someone's life in a positive way and that value is returned to you with an increase in your bank account.

Your product should speak directly to your target market, which you should now know inside and out. You should know if they like audio or video consumption, text or live Q&A with you. You should know the target market flaws, such as laziness or chasing opportunities without focus, but also be able to provide them the magic bullet to get their desired results.

For my New Music Economy product, I knew that independent musicians were usually struggling to make ends meet, great with certain types of technology (like guitar pedals and recording software) and did not have the means to pay large deposits for thousands of CD's or t-shirts.

So, my product played off their weaknesses and turned them into strengths. I showed them how to create instant online income by recreating an old product and repackaging it, then selling it using PayPal. I walked them through the drop-shipping process for ordering CD's and t-shirts, so their fans paid them before the CD was printed and shipped. And I gave them the resources for technology that enabled them to use drag-and-drop visual cues to manage the technical side.

In order to create a winning online course, you need to know the psychology of your market clients and help them to overcome their weaknesses and turn them into strengths. This is the key technique for creating a product that not only gets sold, but gets attention from the marketplace, stands the test of time and helps you create a long-term business – by using your knowledge and creating a platform to help people change their lives.

It is a big undertaking, but as a digital entrepreneur, it is your responsibility to use your knowledge to help people.

One last piece of advice that I will never forget is that: "You don't need to be a 'perfect 10' to teach a '1.' You only need to be a '2.' " You always have someone that you can help and they will reward you for that help. Over time, as you teach and help others you will likely grow into a '10' out of the sheer fact that you are living and breathing that industry daily, gaining experience and touching so many people's lives with your product.

So, get out there and start making products. Once you set your first product into the market, you will want to continue and increase the value you provide. To this day, I get no greater joy than creating something where someone tells me it helped them elevate their business, their life or their relationships.

About Greg

Greg Rollett is an Emmy® Award-Winning Producer, Best-Selling Author and Marketing Expert who works with experts, authors and entrepreneurs all over the world. He utilizes the power of new media, direct response and personality-driven marketing to attract more clients and to create more freedom in the businesses and lives of his clients.

After creating a successful string of his own educational products and businesses, Greg began helping others in the production and marketing of their own products and services.

Greg has written for *Mashable, Fast Company, Inc.com, the Huffington Post, AOL, AMEX's Open Forum* and others, and continues to share his message helping experts and entrepreneurs grow their business through marketing.

He has co-authored Best-Selling books with Jack Canfield, Dan Kennedy, Brian Tracy, Tom Hopkins, James Malinchak, Robert Allen, Ryan Lee and many other leading experts from around the world.

Greg's client list includes Michael Gerber, Brian Tracy, Tom Hopkins, Sally Hogshead, Coca-Cola, Miller Lite and Warner Brothers, along with thousands of entrepreneurs and small-business owners across the world. Greg's work has been featured on FOX News, ABC, NBC, CBS, CNN, *USA Today, Inc Magazine, Fast Company, The Wall Street Journal, The Daily Buzz* and more.

To contact Greg, pls visit:
- http://ambitious.com
- greg@ambitious.com

CHAPTER 6

HARNESSING THE POWER IN YOUR GUT

BY "JOHNNY B" - JOHN BRETTHAUER

ROOT COMMAND

Sparked from the germ of life and crafted from a blend of stardust, you are a miracle.

Through a 4-billion-year struggle in the crucible of evolutionary mortal combat, your "design" has survived. You are a work in progress – a "Live Photo" in the arc of life.

Surviving long enough to have children, who then survive long enough to procreate, is evolutionary success. This means that your blueprints are passed on. All life has evolved around this root command: SURVIVE!

The instinct to survive predates language. Primitive compulsive focus can suspend and overwhelm all other concerns. This predisposition can be hijacked through marketing, games, drugs, manipulation, and most commonly the random events in our lives. It can also be harnessed and is the power behind man's greatest achievements.

FEELING YOUR WAY

My emotions soared as my first son was born. His tiny life was literally in my hands as he stretched his leg up and his arm to the side. He seemed to reach for the limits of his expanded world.

I would never be the same.

Our brains reward behaviors, experiences and thoughts with "feel good" hormones [oxytocin in this case] to convey innate survival instincts. This situational guidance reaches across generations and passes information through the evolutionary branches of life.

Oxytocin promotes cuddling and social bonding. The *addictive quality* of this compulsive guidance system is a survival advantage. A cooperative group is more effective than a group of "me-first" competitors.

Oxytocin is one of many *addictive* guidance systems. While these systems have helped mankind survive, they can also foster destructive compulsions, bringing unwelcome suffering through addictive and disempowering habits of all kinds, such as drugs, alcohol, crippling fear, reckless investments, high-risk behaviors, etc.

These guidance systems have a powerful effect on us, are largely unconscious and seemingly out of our control.

MISALIGNED CORE VALUES

After meeting the love of my life, I took a job as an insurance agent. I was a California boy confronted by 20-degrees-below-zero weather. With no coat, no gloves, no shoes (only slippers), and a broken heater in my car, I was undaunted. I was driven by my passion to earn money for my sweetheart and to protect my clients from devastating financial ruin. Because I was aligned with my core values, I found the inner drive to repeatedly break office records and eventually set a new world record for company sales.

Then I heard from a customer that his claim had been denied, when I firmly believed *my* company should have paid out.

I obsessed over this injustice. My emotions raged from disbelief, anger and incongruence, to sorrow, exhaustion and sadness.

I still wanted to make money for my family, but I could no longer sell *their* policy. I was sick to my stomach at the thought of returning to work. My gut was speaking. In fact, it was shouting.

A misalignment with your core values puts you in chaos and unbearable pain. Your potential is blocked.

Hell on earth is pushing with force-of-will, while every cell of your body is screaming in pain – pulling you back into alignment with your core values. You are fighting who you are. If you ignore your gut, eventually your performance will suffer.

You have one foot on the gas and another on the brake. I bet you have felt this. . .

ALIGNING YOUR MISSION TO YOUR CORE VALUES

You are more powerful than you know.

Your subconscious does the heavy lifting. It stealthily influences and edits your awareness and feelings. Computation is happening in every cell and every nested subsystem of your body – not just your brain.

The mind includes every cell. This internal orchestration relies on a distributed system of computation that is largely unconscious and massively parallel.

Your Reticular Activating System is a small part of your brain that acts as a sensory filter to keep the conscious mind from being overwhelmed with massive streams of data. Your subconscious deletes, edits and intensifies your perceptions, feelings and thoughts to sync with your core values, beliefs and mission.

A mind aligned with core values is untethered from the mundane as it summons unrealized reservoirs of strength, persistence and supernatural flow.

I went through an exercise that was fairly intense. It asked a lot of 'why' questions. My core values revolve around being fair and trusting, competence, showing empathy and being a winner.
~ Sam Alkharrat, Global Chief Operating Officer, SAP

You are driven by the yearning and compulsion that emanates from your gut. Your core values have the power to compel or terminate your life's forward motion, trigger powerful gut feelings and unleash your full power.

I believe that "burnout" is not really fatigue; it is the exhaustion of fighting yourself. It is a fight you can't win!

IDENTIFYING YOUR CORE VALUES

First, identify your core values. Then, make your business decisions in sync with your values: hire by them, and fire by them.

To get you started, here are my Personal and Business Core Values. I also keep a list of lessons learned. My lists evolve over time:

Personal Core Values:
- Seeds – Plant Good Seeds and Change *The* World
- Gratitude – Be Grateful and *My* World Changes
- Kindness – Be Kind to Everyone I Meet

- Comfort – Be Sensitive to the Feelings and Comfort of Others
- Love – Express Love, Appreciation and Attention
- Pay It Forward – Make a Brighter Future for Everyone
- Integrity – Live *With* Integrity
- Curiosity – Find a Better Way
- Improve – Be Competent Through Constant Training and Improvement
- No Gurus – Test All Teachings, No Blind Faith
- Compassion – Have Compassion for All Life

Business Core Values:
- Family – Adopt and Care for Clients As If They Are My Own Sons
- WOW! – Deliver "WOW!" Experiences Through Service
- Transparency – Build Open and Honest Relationships
- Kaizen – Embrace Constantly Accelerating Change
- Passion – Embrace the Task at Hand
- Mentors – Invest 10% of My Annual Income to Study Under World-Class Mentors

Core Concepts (the valuable concepts that I don't want to forget):
- Karma Marketing – We Create Top-of-Mind Awareness by Helping and Educating Our Prospects and Clients
- Avid Fans – Each Team Member's Personal Mission is to Create Avid Fans
- Student – Be a Student and Not a Follower
- Advice – Sustain a World-Class Advisory Board
- 80/20 Principle – To Maximize Effectiveness
- Leadership is Flexible – Whoever is in a Position to Lead to a Better Outcome, Must Speak Up and Lead
- Harm No One – Everyone Deserves Protection
- Win-Win – We Create and Nurture Win-Win Relationships with Clients and Vendors
- Referrals – Earning Referrals is a Cornerstone of Our Success

- Seeds – Support Positive Inspirational Messages Through Writing, Art, Movies, Personal Actions, etc.
- Be a Force for Good

Take the time to thoughtfully identify and write your Core Values. Keep the list handy, read it frequently (to program your subconscious) and you will awaken the resourceful giant inside of you.

SUBCONSCIOUS ATHLETICS

Your subconscious is an autonomous force *controlling* your perceptions, decisions and actions. It is self-assembling, using inputs from your most powerful experiences, feelings, visualization, and conscious focus. The more emotionally charged, intense, repeated and powerful the thought, the stronger the impression is on the subconscious.

Imagine a football player running down the field, evading blocks, calculating the path of the ball, catching it, evading tackles and running into the end zone. Touchdown!!!

Forgetting all about the discipline, training, mental and physical toughness – it seems simple until you imagine coordinating 37 trillion cells, evading 11 elite athletes who want to tackle you, and moving the ball towards the end zone. Your mind is also dealing with impulses of fight-or-flight, fear, ego, career, health and family concerns. You don't have the time to consider each muscle. In reality, many of them cannot be fired individually. Yet each one is constantly adjusted by angle, speed and force: the result of careful physical and mental training.

This is the magic of training and chunking. Individual movements are chunked into useful clusters. They are triggered by what just happened and what is expected to happen. Yet thousands of adjustments must be made in real time for competitive success. This is way too much data for you to consciously monitor and control.

THE FLOW OR BEING IN THE ZONE

The Flow is the suspension of conscious micromanagement. The conscious mind sets the goal and steps out of control, but remains vigilantly focused as a silent observer during execution. The body responds as if controlled by a supernatural force. The subconscious controls which options you become aware of, selects the options before you realize what they are, and makes countless decisions while you are in motion. It manages your perception, determination, confidence and execution.

Training the body is vital, but it is not enough. You must also train your subconscious to manage perceptions, awareness, focus and resources to deliver peak performance in a complex real-world setting.

FLOW IN YOUR BUSINESS

Have you ever missed an obvious opportunity, failed to say the right thing, or failed to perceive the critical factor?

I know I have.

If you say something that you didn't mean, who said it? Why was it said?

Have you ever shouted in privacy, "WHY? WHY? WHY?" Yet with a slight shift it would have gone so differently. In fact, the alternative path was even easier to execute and infinitely more rewarding.

Our days appear to be a stream of unexpected random events. We bump into each one and are affected emotionally. We may make some reactionary response. But we are also changed by our experiences. There is no coherent direction in this model, so there is no progress.

Meanwhile, our Reticular Activating System is busy subconsciously deleting the vast majority of our perceptions. Most sensory inputs are invisible to us.

The mind will delete all input that is not consistent with your fully-implanted mission and core values.

I'm sure you've also seen people with the 'Midas Touch'. Everything they do looks so easy, so profitable and unbelievably successful.

There is a Flow in business as well. It's that exhilarating state where you are inclined to say, "I can do no wrong. I'm untouchable. I'm on fire!" And Flow looks effortless because all the training gives you the capacity, the mental work gives you the split-second execution, and the result looks like poetry.

If only we could bottle that . . . and we can!

Flow feels like the invisible hand of God is orchestrating the universe and your actions, revealing a wonderful synchronicity – a dance with the Divine.

THE ROLE OF THE CONSCIOUS MIND

Without conscious direction and subconscious alignment, life is like a pinball bouncing off the bumpers and being "paddled" until you fall off the board.

Most people's moods are reflections of whom they meet, how they are treated or what happens to them during the day. They are thrust into the day with no plan, no goal and no mission. There is a sense of victimhood in being knocked around with no real progress towards an outcome of your choosing. At best, you are a pawn in someone else's game, or worse . . .

Only the conscious mind can identify a goal or a worthwhile mission that extends beyond the horizon of the day.

SETTING GOALS

We overestimate the progress we can make in a day, but underestimate the compound effect of pursuing a consistent goal over a period of time.

It is only by persistent steps in a defined direction that we can travel a great distance. Your goal defines your destination and direction. Your persistent conscious training imprints your goal into your subconscious mind to facilitate your defined mission. By taking daily action towards your goal, your subconscious guides your awareness, passion and actions. This process releases your full potential.

You are not fully alive unless you are in alignment with your Core Values and moving towards a defined outcome that allows you to harness your full arsenal of resources.

Without a goal, your subconscious has no mission. No one can help you get to a place you haven't identified. You are lost in a game with no meaning.

It is very tough to keep a long-term goal or mission top of mind for a prolonged period of time. I typically keep the ultimate dream / goal in my subconscious and even doing so, I see my daily decisions and actions helping me inch towards the goal.

I am able to remind myself of these long-term goals through quarterly self-reviews that I do at the beginning of each quarter, where I evaluate how far away I am from where I need to be. I do an annual review on the last day of each year as well. Oftentimes, it is also fun to see where I was 10 years or 5 years ago and how far I've come.

Also, it is very important to pick goals that do not change frequently, which means it is something that is worthy of dedicating one's life towards. Everything tactical to getting there I'm flexible about.

~ Wook Chung, Director, Product Management at Twitter

The purpose of a goal is to remove yourself from being a pawn in your own life. You gain control and resonate with confidence. By establishing a goal, you create a blueprint for programming and syncing with your entire being. With prolonged consistency punctuated by self-reviews, you can move mountains.

ACTION SUMMARY

By setting goals in alignment with your core values and programming your subconscious, you will tap into the entirety of your resources. This needs to be sustained with a daily practice that *recruits* and *keeps* your subconscious on the job.

There are many ways to direct your own programming through your daily/weekly/quarterly practice: OKRs, bookending your day, reviewing goals, morning huddles, visualization, coaches, classes, vision boards, and many more are all effective. For the best effect, blend in vivid senses, strong emotions and repetition during your entire mission and you will recruit your subconscious.

With consistent mental work and by taking concrete actions in the direction of your mission, you will avoid inner struggle, live a more harmonious life, achieve amazing results and be a force for good in the world.

In this state of Flow, you will experience exhilaration. Then you become free. You no longer work for money. Instead, you work for joy, contribution, and significance. Being fully present on this path is deeply gratifying.

Can you imagine a world of brothers and sisters exhilarated in Flow, as they contribute to a better world? May you choose to plant the seeds around you for the crop you want to harvest!

Happy trails my friend . . .

[Further inspiration and guidance can be drawn from the following exemplary work: *The Success Principles*(TM) by Jack Canfield.]

About Johnny B

"Johnny B" - John Bretthauer is a Best-Selling Author®
and Silicon Valley's Favorite REALTOR®.

Johnny B was also named as one of America's Premier
Experts® in recognition of his experience and success in
real estate. This happened in August of 2012, following his appearance as
a guest on America's Premier Experts, a television show designed to help
the public make sound choices when buying or selling homes, filmed in
Washington, D.C. and aired on ABC, NBC, CBS and Fox affiliates.

In 2013, Johnny B joined a select group of America's leading real estate
experts to co-write a book titled, *The Ultimate HomeBuyer's Guide: The
Nation's Leading Expert Advisors Reveal Their Secrets of Success for Buying
Right in Any Market.* On the day of release, *The Ultimate HomeBuyer's Guide*
achieved best-seller status in six Amazon.com categories. In 2013, Johnny B
was accepted into the National Academy of Best-Selling Authors®.

Additionally, he has joined with other best-selling authors, CelebrityPress®
Publishing and the Entrepreneurs International Foundation to become a
"Village Sponsor" of the Global Learning XPRIZE® Initiative.

Johnny B was invited by Realtor.com® to speak at the Annual RE/MAX R4
Convention in 2014 and received great reviews from several industry leaders
for his insight into marketing and customer service in today's real estate
industry. His Bay Area radio show, *Real Estate Rumble,* was aired in Silicon
Valley on KDOW and KNEW to provide the public with real estate information
and protection.

He is a Master Certified Negotiation Expert, a Certified International Property
Specialist and has earned the designation of Graduate, REALTOR® Institute.
His passion is supporting his clients' success in buying and selling their most
valuable and sensitive asset – their home.

Johnny B is a passionate supporter of success in many areas. He is a Charter
Member of the International Academy of Filmmakers and produced three
films in 2017, to support the message of foremost thought leaders with the
likes of Rudy Ruettiger (inspiration for the Hollywood Blockbuster "Rudy"),

Brian Tracy (author of more than 70 books and world-famous trainer to 5,000,000 participants) and Jack Canfield (featured in the popular movie "The Secret" and creator of the "Chicken Soup for the Soul" series).

Johnny B is the proud father of two sons, and spends his spare time with his lovely wife Vicki, and their two cats, Teenie and Monkey.

To learn more about Johnny B, please visit:
- www.JohnnyB.com
- www.MeetJohnnyB.com

Coldwell Banker - CalBRE# 01480256

CHAPTER 7

SOCIAL MEDIA MASTERY

BY LINDSAY DICKS

You Don't Have to be an Expert in Social Media
To be an Expert on Social Media

Do you have what it takes to be a success on social media? Maybe you're comfortable with Facebook and don't see the value in any of the dozens of other social media sites out there. Perhaps you've dabbled in other sites like Twitter and Instagram, but don't want to waste time on them. Let me tell you, you could be passing up a great opportunity to boost your career.

You don't need to be on social media, just like you don't need air conditioning. Isn't life better with it, though? Here's the litmus test: if you have a website, social media will make it better. It will make your site work harder for you. It will make you stand out in a sea of competitors.

Increased traffic to your website isn't the only way you can make money off the Internet. If you do it right, and become popular enough on social media, you can generate revenue directly from your social media content.

You're probably thinking, sure, easy for her to say. She's in the business. It's her job. You're right, it is my job, and I'm pretty darn good at it. That's how I know you can be successful on social media. To help you understand your potential, let me give you an idea of the audience social media has on the Internet.

Facebook: 1 billion+ users – Five new Facebook profiles are created every second.
YouTube: 1 billion+ viewers – The top YouTuber is PewDiePie, with over 54 million subscribers.
Instagram: 600 million+ users – Instagram users share over 95 million photos and videos every day, on average.
Twitter: 300 million+ users – Twitter users send approximately 5,700 tweets every second.

With all those users, how can you make your posts stand out? Facebook, Instagram, and Twitter all use the hashtag symbol # to highlight trending topics. Here are some of the most popular hashtags on the Internet from 2016:

Facebook:
#love
#photooftheday
#happy

Instagram:
#photooftheday
#tbt
#followme

Twitter:
#Rio2016
#PokemonGo
#GameOfThrones

As you can see, Facebook and Instagram have similar types of hashtags, you might say timeless, while Twitter is much more topical. If you want to get noticed, a good way to become more visible is to jump on the bandwagon, or to be more precise, jump on the hashtag. Is there a hashtag you can take advantage of? Reese's captured a whopping 73% of total engagement on Facebook and Twitter with the hashtag: #MarchMood.

You probably won't get that kind of result, but the trick is to find a trending hashtag that relates to you or your business. You can keep track of the latest hashtags on a free site like hashtags.org to see which ones are up, down, or remain constant. Keep an eye on trending topics to see when there's something relevant you can post on.

So, that gives you an idea of how you can reach people, but the real secret of social media is having people come to you. Luckily, you don't have to figure that out on your own. There are already people on the Internet with a dedicated following.

Rise of the Influencers
I know, it sounds like a sci-fi movie, right? This is where you get serious on social media. Let's start by defining just what makes a person an influencer. An influencer is someone who is an expert in their field, and has the knowledge and charisma to attract an audience with similar interests.

At what point does a person with followers become an influencer? There isn't a demarcation line that you can cross over to officially be labelled an influencer. Here's what I say: if people are coming to you for your opinion, you're an influencer. In fact, a study by Augure found that 79 percent of respondents feel social media influencers should express their opinions in their posts.

The beauty of the influencer role on social media is how they're able to speak directly to their followers. There's no filter between the person and the audience. To be an effective influencer, you must gain the trust of your followers. You're not doing an infomercial. Forget about "set it and forget it." Now that's not to say you can't be compensated for highlighting a product or service. There are influencers who accept payment for using a particular product or service, but you have to be upfront about it.

I could write a whole other chapter explaining how being on social media can create a synergy that can snowball into a successful career. However, let me show you how you can harness the power of social media by taking a closer look at a real influencer.

A Study in Art

First, let me tell you how I found our influencer. I asked my friend's daughter, Claire, who she follows on social media. Her favorite YouTuber is Baylee Jae, an artist who works with markers to create beautiful works of art. Baylee has almost 800,000 subscribers who watch her engaging tutorials and demonstrations. She has uploaded over 250 videos to the site, as well as posting a daily vlog. Her Instagram account also has over 100,000 followers.

Some of her most popular videos include the 3-marker challenge, where she picks three markers at random and has to complete a drawing using only those three colors. It's both an interesting and fun concept. Baylee's tool of choice is Copic markers. Now, if you go on YouTube and type in "Baylee Jae Copic Addiction," you'll see just how many of the markers she has. In the video, she talks about her obsession with purchasing and drawing with the markers. She really believes in the product and uses them to create her artwork.

OK, so we've met Baylee, now let's take a look at how she parlays her influence into a successful career for herself. The two sites that work best for her are YouTube and Twitter. With YouTube, she's able to share her videos and tutorials with her followers, and Twitter allows her to quickly post about her latest work and catch up with people she follows in the online art community.

There are several ways she generates income directly from her social media sites. She places ads on her YouTube videos with Google Adsense, which produces a significant amount of income for her. She also accepts sponsors for some of her videos, but she announces it at the beginning of the video so she doesn't betray the trust of her audience. Baylee also likes to livestream video on the website, Twitch, that generates ad revenue and subscription fees for her.

YouTube, Twitter, and Facebook all have links back to her website so she can create more traffic and income for the site. Baylee's website has an online store where she sells her creations in many forms – stickers, t-shirts, cellphone cases, and other products.

We can now see how Baylee's taken her expertise and influence to create a successful career for herself. But let's not forget about Copic markers. My friend tells me Claire has over two dozen Copic markers, and the company didn't have to pay a dime in advertising.

Be the Influencer

Now that we've seen a social media influencer in action, the question is, how can you become one? Starting your quest for social media success isn't just about sitting in front of your iPhone and talking about the latest gossip. You first have to determine what field you want to concentrate on. Don't try to be a jack of all trades and a master of none. Find your niche. Do you want to focus on your professional skills, a hobby, or lifestyle trends?

Once you've decided on your vocation, it's time to get down to work. Here are some steps you can take to get your social media career on track:

Do your research – See what other people are saying and posting online about your area of expertise. Read blogs pertaining to your specialty, and utilize Google Alerts to stay abreast of topics. Don't be afraid to reach out to bloggers and influencers for guidance and support. Networking is a great way to learn more about how to become successful on social media. It's been my experience that online communities really band together to help each other out.

Prioritize – You can't be everywhere at once. To maximize your time on social media, decide which sites work best for you, and get the most responses, and concentrate on those. If you want to prosper, you need to post consistently, and you can't do that if you spread yourself too thin. Baylee has tried lots of different social media sites, but spends most of her time on YouTube, Facebook, Twitter, and Instagram because that's where her audience is.

Keep your content fresh – Sure, people love to watch Seinfeld reruns, but you're no Kramer. You've got to continually update your social media content to attract new followers and keep current ones. Your research will help you stay abreast of latest trends in your industry that you can talk about and provide your insight and advice on.

Put a face to a name – Don't hide behind your posts. If you want to make an impact on social media, you need to do more than just posting comments on Facebook or Twitter. Three of the most important parts of being a social media star are video, video, and video. It's one of the leading tools of engagement on social media. People want to see you talk about your topics, not just read them. Don't have experience with editing and uploading videos? Don't worry. There are plenty of editing programs out there with online tutorials that can walk you through the process step-by-step.

Listen to feedback – Your followers often tell you what they want to see and read. Look through the comments section to see what people like and tailor your content to their preferences. Take the time to interact with your audience. Who knows? Your next topic could be sitting in your inbox.

It's about time – Many people take up social media expecting to make a big splash and earn loads of money overnight, and then reality sets in. It takes time to put together videos, write blogs, respond to your followers, and all the other parts that go along with being on social media. According to Baylee, social media has to be a passion, and it takes more work than most people realize.

Be realistic – You need to have some realistic expectations going into your endeavor. You're probably not going to get a thousand subscribers overnight. It's going to take time to grow your audience, so focus on the quality of the people you have following you, rather than the number.

Treat it like a business – If you want to get serious about your social media success, you need to dedicate as much time to it as you would any other business. Think strategically and put together a business plan with goals and deadlines. It will help you focus your energies in the right places.

You Have What it Takes

There are many qualities that make a successful social media influencer. You have to be knowledgeable about your subject, passionate about your content, and able to communicate your thoughts and ideas to people in an engaging manner. Sounds like you, doesn't it?

Don't expect to be an overnight success. Just like any other endeavor, social media stardom isn't guaranteed. It can be difficult to break through and create an army of followers. You'll probably face a few hurdles along the way and that may slow you down. The secret is to just keep going. You have all the tools you need to be an online success. All it takes is time, patience, and some social media savvy.

About Lindsay

Lindsay Dicks helps her clients tell their stories in the online world. Being brought up around a family of marketers, but a product of Generation Y, Lindsay naturally gravitated to the new world of on-line marketing. Lindsay began freelance writing in 2000 and soon after launched her own PR firm that thrived by offering an in-your-face "Guaranteed PR" that was one of the first of its type in the nation.

Lindsay's new media career is centered on her philosophy that "people buy people." Her goal is to help her clients build a relationship with their prospects and customers. Once that relationship is built and they learn to trust them as the expert in their field, then they will do business with them. Lindsay also built a proprietary process that utilizes social media marketing, content marketing and search engine optimization to create online "buzz" for her clients that helps them to convey their business and personal story. Lindsay's clientele spans the entire business map and ranges from doctors and small business owners to Inc. 500 CEOs.

Lindsay is a graduate of the University of Florida. She is the CEO of CelebritySites™, an online marketing company specializing in social media and online personal branding. Lindsay is recognized as one of the top online marketing experts in the world and has co-authored more than 25 best-selling books alongside authors such as Steve Forbes, Richard Branson, Brian Tracy, Jack Canfield (creator of the *Chicken Soup for the Soul* series), Dan Kennedy, Robert Allen, Dr. Ivan Misner (founder of BNI), Jay Conrad Levinson (author of the *Guerilla Marketing* series), Leigh Steinberg and many others, including the breakthrough hit *Celebrity Branding You!*

She has also been selected as one of America's PremierExperts™ and has been quoted in *Forbes, Newsweek, The Wall Street Journal, USA Today*, and *Inc.* magazine as well as featured on NBC, ABC, and CBS television affiliates – speaking on social media, search engine optimization and making more money online. Lindsay was also recently brought on FOX 35 News as their Online Marketing Expert.

Lindsay, a national speaker, has shared the stage with some of the top speakers in the world, including Brian Tracy, Lee Milteer, Ron LeGrand,

Arielle Ford, Leigh Steinberg, Dr. Nido Qubein, Dan Sullivan, David Bullock, Peter Shankman and many others. Lindsay was also a Producer on the Emmy-winning film, *Jacob's Turn*, and sits on the advisory board for the Global Economic Initiative.

You can connect with Lindsay at:
- Lindsay@CelebritySites.com
- www.twitter.com/LindsayMDicks
- www.facebook.com/LindsayDicks

CHAPTER 8

SOUL OF SALES
THE NINE UNIVERSAL LAWS

BY ROHIT BASSI

*For, after all, the best thing one can do when it is raining
is let it rain.*
~ Henry Wadsworth Longfellow

Susan Jeffers most amazing book, *Feel the Fear & Do It Anyway*® has been very helpful to the development of many people, including my own. Her work has certainly guided me in doing what I do for a living. Other key influences in my development have been the likes of His Holiness the Dalai Lama, Jack Canfield and Dr. Wayne Dyer.

For many of you out there, selling could be a frightful experience and you refuse to go down this path. The truth of the matter is that no matter what you do, be it getting a job, convincing someone to go out with you on a date, or winning a business deal all involves selling.

When I started my consultancy firm, I had to learn to sell. I coach school and university students, professors, professionals, business owners and many others in the art of public speaking and presentation skills. In this regard, two people, Craig Chapman and Chayya Sakhuja helped me to overcome my fear of educating others. In order for people and organisations to use my services, I had to persuade them to buy from me. This selling effort was not only scary; it also made me feel 'yuck.'

You see, many people say salespeople are liars; they are the scum of the earth and out to make a quick buck. I, too, was of that opinion until I taught myself to view sales as a tool to help others. Here, I must give credit to Jeffrey Gitomer and Arjun Aiyar – both of whom taught me to discern a 'hard' sell from a 'heart' sell. The selling profession is despised by many and is perceived as being aggressive and ruthless.

Even for me, the journey of sales has been daunting and like a path leading into the unknown. The one thing that is known however, is the dynamic nature of the market, technology and trends. The only constant in sales is change. Thus, as a sales professional, you need to be adaptable, flexible and versatile. I would contend that there is one more constant in sales. And that constant is trust. The unsuccessful sales person has most likely underestimated the significance of trust. It is from this foundation that I discovered the soul of sales.

Over the years, I have coached and trained people in the art of public speaking and presentation skills. Surprisingly, in doing so, I have had new and old salespeople ask me to assist them on how to pitch themselves, improve their sales, up their client-relationship management and better communicate with their clients.

To all those who are in sales or are afraid to venture into sales, please allow me to take you into the practical journey I call: *"Soul of Sales – The Nine Universal Laws."* Here they are:

1. **Awareness** – One of my teachers, Dr Segu Ramesh, says, "When you focus you move into attention, this leads to awareness, thus allowing you to get things done with greater

ease." A key called awareness opens the first door to sales success. When you amplify your awareness, you realise that accomplishment in sales is all about service excellence. It is critical for you to know that the only reason you are in your role is because of the customers you serve. Sales cannot exist without service. In other words, a salesperson needs, and has to be, *customer focused* rather than transaction focused. You are correct in thinking that without the transaction the business will stop. However, without the customer, the business will be non-existent, i.e., it will be dead. As a salesperson, your role is about creating a positive customer experience and a journey that is both memorable and appreciated. When you create such an experience and journey, you enter the realm of Soul-Based Service Excellence. In doing so, you are shifting yourself from a transaction and creating an emotional connection of trust and respect with your customers.

2. **Acceptance** – Many people run away from selling, as they are afraid of failure. The two things that hold people back in sales success is rejection and belief that 'no one will buy from me.' Firstly, accept that you will need to regularly educate yourself in order to overcome self-sabotage and limiting beliefs. This is the key to on-going success. Secondly, accept that your service/product may not be suitable for everyone, so be clear of your market. Not everyone is your customer. Thirdly, accept that you are forever in learning and development mode. There will be days or even weeks when inspiration is low and motivation is dead. You will be rejected, as well as beaten to a pulp both mentally and emotionally. Many times, fear will cloud your vision. The only way to overcome your fears and pass through the dark-side is to accept that this is a part of the sales success journey. By doing so, in addition, in developing yourself you are also developing trust and respect with customers.

3. **Compassion** – "Ruthless Compassion" is a phrase regularly

used in the business world. It is it sad to see how so-called business leaders, sales leaders and sales people show their ruthless actions by hiding behind such a pathetic phrase. It is these toxic individuals who may truly prove fatal to others, the organisation and to their own lives. Compassion is not about having pity on others. It has nothing to do with being nice and feeling sorry for others. It also has nothing to do with being disrespectful to yourself or being a 'yes' person to the needs and wants of others. In simple terms, it is about being loving, empowering, tolerant and forgiving. It is about being respectful to yourself and to others. It is about setting aside your ego. For the users of "Ruthless Compassion," please view the Ted Talk by Daniel Goleman (author of *Emotional Intelligence*) "Why aren't we more compassionate?" As a salesperson, compassion allows you to know your client better and genuinely connects you with them. There is no room for 'fake-it-till-you-make-it' in sales.

4. **Passion** – Whether you are a sales novice or veteran, watch the movie *Glengarry Glen Ross*. You will learn about the famous sales technique called ABC (Always Be Closing). This technique is about "Fear Sales" and "Reward Sales." It is an extremely self-centred and selfish technique and is a far cry from being client-focused. Passion is all about Always Be Caring (ABC) for the client, yourself and the business you work for. It is about paying close attention to the UPB (Unique Perceived Benefit—a phrase coined by The Marketing Guild) of the client. You are there to provide help and guide the client - enabling them to make a good decision when it comes to getting a product/service that will fulfil their immediate needs or will benefit them in the long run. The total focus is to develop a solution that gets the client into a comfort zone where they see a light at the end of the tunnel. "Passion Sales" allows you to connect with your core values of serving clients as a trusted advisor. The journey is not about a transaction. Instead, it is about forging a successful ethical relationship, which allows both you and

the client to be in a win-win situation in the short, medium and long run.

5. **Assertiveness** – Sales managers, directors and gurus often use words to be aggressive with your sales, or they say you need to dominate the market. These phrases are a cringe factor for many and the energy around it comes across as creepy and untrustworthy. Psychologist Kendra Cherry, defines aggression as "a range of behaviours that can result in both physical and psychological harm to oneself, other or objects in the environment." Such an interaction could lead to harming another person, either physically or mentally. In sales terms, this means to win/succeed by hook or by crook, there is no mercy. When it comes to assertiveness, Dorland's Medical Dictionary defines it as "a form of behaviour characterized by a confident declaration or affirmation of a statement without need of proof; this affirms the person's rights or point of view without either aggressively threatening the rights of another (assuming a position of dominance) or submissively permitting another to ignore or deny one's rights or point of view." I prefer the assertive sales route any day. It was Chayya Sakhuja who taught me that sales have nothing to do with aggression. Instead, sales are about connecting with the client, overcoming rejection, remaining focused, doing your best and having an assertive outlook in all situations.

6. **Gratitude** – With faith and trust your client gives you a precious gift. That precious gift is their time and attention. It is an amazing feeling to receive this gift from your clients. Yet many of us take the client for granted. Inadvertently, we could abuse the client's time. As Rick Warren says, "Time is your most precious gift because you only have a set amount of it." Anyone in sales needs to have an attitude of gratitude. Whomever you connect with in sales, always remember to thank them for their time. No matter if a sale never happens, always be thankful. My dear friend and coach, Ray Jacobs,

continues to reinforce in me the power of gratitude. Ray has been empowering people at all levels for over 40 years now.

7. **Value** – On numerous occasions, I have been told to value my service. I would simply brush the advice away. Ramez Helou, an exceptional sales trainer, awaked me to the importance of value. He taught me that value goes beyond the price that we place on a product/service. In this regard, one fine day I saw a friend's social media comment. She was in the midst of a challenging situation with the pricing of her services. She was upset because a client wanted to reduce her price even though they openly appreciated her quality of work. Now, that was a difficult place for her to be in; it is like helping someone get up when they have fallen, and once you have picked them up you simply push them down again. To cut a long story short, she stuck to her guns and behold the client agreed to continue working with her at the original price. This is a lesson in having belief, trust and knowing the value that you offer through your work. Remember, if you are being undervalued and choose to walk away, then do so with grace rather than arrogance. Be respectful at all times, and do your best to maintain the relationship. Release your ego and put aside judgements.

8. **Communication** – My father in law would always say: as long as the other person understands your message like you would like them to understand it, that means you have successfully communicated with them. The foundation, the building block, the essence of all that we do is based on our communication. You are always communicating. Even our act of silence is a form of communication. You consciously or unconsciously decide how to communicate with yourself and others. Yes, at times it is tough communicating your message and you may want to give up. Communication happens through various media such as verbal (language, words, sentences), non-verbal (body language, gestures, emotions) and voice (tone, pace, volume). Writing is

another element of communication. The most critical aspect of communication however, is how you communicate within yourself. When a person is unable to communicate with him or herself in a positive and productive manner, then the outcomes usually are unpleasant. Your ability to communicate with yourself is crucial. Thereafter, it only gets easier to communicate with others. This is what is known as rapport. Rapport is all about creating the essence of trust, respect, understanding and cooperation, all of which begins within you. Communication involves the use of all of your senses consciously. Be impeccable in your communication at all times, even when you are off the sales stage.

9. **Rejection** – My parents were right in saying that rejection takes place in every phase of one's life. For me, some of the most amazing people are those who overcome rejection. It is phenomenal how they take a rejection or a "NO" as the *"Next Opportunity."* Every rejection is a learning opportunity and simply leads to development. One of the greatest challenges that you will face in sales is rejection. Rejection may cause you to doubt your own abilities. Some of you may view a rejection as your worst nightmare. The evolved sales professional says, "Rejection is divine redirection towards something beautiful beyond your imagination." For most of us, rejection after rejection lands great blows to our confidence. We feel the devastation deep within ourselves. The feeling of lack drowns us and we are unable to comprehend the so-called divine plan that is unfolding for us. In the moment of rejection, and beyond that moment, nothing makes sense. Our negative emotions override so-called common sense. A thick layer of misery and self-pity engulfs us. No matter how painful the experience, there is that someone who tells us "we are where we are meant to be." We are told to have that trust in the universe and know that everything will be just fine. Apply this principle. Take a leap of faith in sales.

Being persistent in sales is great. Remember, some could easily view this as desperation or even pressuring someone to buy something from you – if done without finesse. Even though I coach people in the art of public speaking and presentation skills, I am still required to sell my services. For me selling equates to service excellence, being ethical and never forcing someone into buying something that they have no need for.

Now, look at the laws again carefully. You will realise these nine laws are also the universal laws of life.

In the caring and encouraging words of the great philosopher Lao Tzu:

Life is a series of natural and spontaneous changes.
Never resist them; that only creates sorrow. Let reality be reality.
Let things flow naturally forward in whatever way they like.

About Rohit

Rohit Bassi is a pro-active and highly-engaging speaker who inspires you through the power of awareness, consciousness and energy. He is a passionate trainer, coach and facilitator in the areas of presentation skills, leadership and management, sales and business development, communication skills and customer service.

His work is about growing from the inside out and being practical in this hectic world we live in. For him, this means connecting with your own inner self to bring balance and integration to outperform yourself.

His Background:
- Born and brought up in London, UK.
- Supported numerous businesses spread across 40 countries.
- International experience across the globe of 20+years.

His Work:
- Specialises in public speaking and presentation skills.
- Delivered sessions to 250,000+ delegates.
- Creator of Soul of Sales & Soul-Based Service Excellence.

His Qualifications:
- B.Sc. (Hons.) in Applied Computing and Business Studies.
- TAP & CIPD, Practitioner in NLP, Reiki, & The Solution.
- Licensed Trainer for *Feel the Fear & Do It Anyway.*®

He is committed to adding value to you using his extensive years of international experience from the United Kingdom, Afghanistan, Congo, Ireland, France, Australia, Vietnam, America, Philippines, India, Kenya and all through the Middle East.

Rohit has delivered sessions to the likes of British Gas, Nielsen, KPMG, PwC, YouGov, Cadbury Schweppes, BAA, Eurostar, Oracle, EMC, VMware, HSBC, Emirates NBD, Abu Dhabi Terminals, Harley-Davidson, Emaar Hospitality, Jumeirah, Marriott, Harrods, DP World and many more.

- YouTube Channel: https://www.youtube.com/user/iaminlearning1
- LinkedIn Profile: https://www.linkedin.com/in/rohitbassi
- Website: http://www.in-learning.com
- rohit@in-learning.com

CHAPTER 9

THE CHANGING FACE OF FACEBOOK

BY JAMES E. DICKS JR.

It's been more than five years now that I have been working with social media marketing. If you are reading this, then no doubt you are looking to increase your success. Let me share with you how I turned my own social media marketing needs into a successful digital/social media agency.

During the great recession in 2008, my financial business was simply crippled by all the excessive financial regulatory oversight. I made a decision to stop doing business in the U.S., as growth in my industry was expanding in double-digit increases abroad, versus the low single digits in the U.S. The decision was obvious, I had to expand my business overseas. At that time, my database was extensive with tens of thousands of people that have used my technology, but they all resided in the U.S. I had virtually no international footprint to start growing my business, and I needed to start marketing overseas.

I had marketed overseas before, but only in countries that my institutional memory was applicable. I have more than 30 years of marketing under my belt, including spending well over a half billion dollars in marketing for the firms that I've worked with on long and short-form television commercials, newsprint, radio, direct mail and magazine advertising. One thing missing was digital media. I had tried Google ads previously, and had moderate success, but my biggest issue was always the scalability of Google ads. I learned long ago that to be successful in any marketing campaign you needed to spend to a diminishing return.

If you have a budget and you get a return of let's say 3:1, well then there is no reason not to spend everything you can until the 3:1 ratio starts decreasing. When that happens, you pull back your spending. The problem is that there are very few marketing avenues that enable you to do that:

- Direct Mail – No, there are only so many addresses that you can buy.
- Radio – A little more.
- Magazines – No.
- Newspapers – no
- Television – Yes, you can always spend more money on more time, and better time slots, to get more eyeballs watching your program.

But today there are so many channels it is much harder to be cost effective and capture an intuitive audience.

I use Facebook, and one of the primary reasons is that it is scalable. There are over 184 billion people around the world on Facebook! Using this platform, I can micro-target my audience, deliver my message and collect their contact information without ever leaving my office. So, that is what I did. I took my business and my message overseas in five languages and built a database of over 24,000 new contacts in less than 12 months using only Facebook.

As I shared those experiences with others, I started getting questions about how I did it and how they can do it too. The next thing I know, fast-forward to today, I have a thriving, successful digital media agency that focuses on Facebook advertising.

I was with a new prospective client the other day and their situation was similar to most reading this. Either you have never advertised on Facebook but have heard about it and are interested in doing some ads, or, like this perspective client I met with, you have been doing some Facebook ads and are struggling. I get a few kinds of replies from this type of experience. The first one is, "James, I need your help, we have been advertising on Facebook and it is just too much for us." Or, "We don't have the resources or the experience to be successful and would like you and your team to do it for us." The other type of comment is, "James, we have been running our own ads on Facebook and they quite frankly did really well. We were killing it and getting hundreds of leads, but for some reason, we are not getting anything now."

Ah, that is the interesting one from many aspects. Facebook is not stupid; they are one of the biggest and most successful technology companies in the world. Yes, they are a social media company, but their extensive understanding of technology drives everything they do on social media and how we use it in our everyday lives. That means they know how to make money, and the way they make money is from people and businesses advertising on Facebook. The secret to successful advertising on Facebook is not necessarily complicated, but it does take an understanding of the metrics and processes.

Facebook is always changing their algorithms so that they can deliver your ads more efficiently and get you the leads at the cost you want; however, the same technology allows them to accomplish their own financial goals that, of course, they have to report to their shareholders. Did you ever think that maybe they know when a new business advertiser comes on board? What if they said, "Hey! Johnny just started running ads for the first time today, let's open up the faucet and make sure he is getting leads at great cost no matter what." Now, what do you think you would do if all of a sudden you were spending $10.00 a day and get 20 leads for $.50 a lead? Yeah, you would increase your ad spend to $20.00 a day, why not? After all, we want to spend our marketing dollars to a diminishing return (scalability) right?

Then, all of a sudden, you start to see your ad metrics getting worse. Facebook has got you sucked in and you're spending more and they are making more. I am not saying that they do this, just asking you to think about it. Just like anything else in life you have to work at, Facebook is no different. I constantly hear that the only thing in life that is certain is death, taxes and Facebook changes. Facebook makes changes to their user interface and algorithms constantly, sometimes many times in a week. You have to stay on top of it. You have to understand things like ad fatigue or relevance scores and where to run ads to avoid competition with Fortune 500 companies, etc.

If you spend the time you will reap the rewards. Facebook ads work, your customer is on Facebook, it does not matter if they are B2B or B2C you can find them and you can micro-target them to be the very specific, qualified lead you want. If you are getting too many leads, you can increase some of the targeting filters such as a person's income, net worth, whether they own or rent a home and just about anything else you can think of. Each time you make those changes to your audience, you will reduce the amount of leads that come through and increase the quality of the lead. Facebook will work for any business, so long as the business is not prohibited from running ads on Facebook. There are only a few industries that are excluded from this kind of advertising; to find out which they are, just go online and search Facebook terms and conditions to make sure your business is not one of those prohibited.

I have yet to find a business that I could not drive leads to. That said, I want to leave you with the number one thing that I find businesses struggle with – which I have personally witnessed from just about all niches out there. When I walk in to see a new client, the theme is always the same, "I need Leads." That's true, and you will get leads from Facebook. However, it will not do you any good to get leads from Facebook if you don't know, or you don't have, a viable product or service to sell.

You would be surprised at how many businesses are trying to get leads when they really don't have anything to sell yet. Seriously, I have clients that have come on board asking me to get them leads, but have absolutely nothing to sell. So make sure you have clearly defined your product or service and what the price point is or will be. From experience, if you are selling a high-ticket item, be prepared to make sure your sales process has a live phone call to the lead in to it. Less than a few hundred and you can utilize an automated process.

The process is actually the other side of most business failures when working with leads: you get the leads, you have something to sell, but you have no process in place to work the leads. I have had customers that I send leads to with a great cost per lead conversion – only to find out that they didn't contact the leads we sent them anyway. You would be surprised at how often this happens. Leads start coming in and then and only then do the clients realize the inefficiencies of their sales process.

To help you do it yourself, and be successful, you can follow a few simple steps that I have outlined below for you:

Step 1 - Identify your product or service and the price points that you want to charge for them. If you are going to have a high price point, let's say $1,000 to $10,000 +, you need to think about having a live sales call during the process. You can use qualifying communication through automation and nurturing, but ultimately, you need a sales person on the phone building a relationship and asking for the sale.

Step 2 - Your process, this is an extension of step one. What will happen to the lead? Will they get a confirmation when they enter your sales pipeline, or do you have a sales pipeline? Will they get a welcome email? How will you notify your sales team that you have a new lead, will you have a follow-up process or nurture sequence to keep your leads engaged?

Step 3 - Set up your ads on Facebook. Make sure that you have a well-thought-out landing page or lead ad, and be sure that all of the notifications in the above steps are working to notify your sales team and/or process of the new lead. Test all the links in the ad process before going live. Be sure to maintain a high relevance score on your ads by having your content on your landing page correlate to the content in your ad. You will get better deliverability by doing so.

These are just three easy steps to get started advertising on Facebook, since I only had a small amount of space to share my passion and excitement about Facebook, and how advertising on Facebook can help make your business much more successful than you ever thought it could be.

Here are a few more thoughts that you can take along with you for further research that will help you become a better Facebook advertiser:

Test various price points: $10.00 a day may be better than $20.00, and $47.00 a day may be better than $20.00, but $50.00 may not be as good as $15.00. The point is that Facebook runs very complicated algorithms and every variable you make or change can affect the overall success of the ad.

Video typically does better than print: Always look for engaging images that create conversation. Make sure that your landing pages are mobile responsive, 84% of the 1.81 billion people are using a mobile operating system on Facebook, don't dismiss this audience group.

Look for ad fatigue: By that, I mean if your ad stops performing, then change it. However, be careful changing ads as it takes about

10 days for Facebook to optimize an ad so that they can deliver the ad to the most likely person to engage with your ad. And, as contradictory as this sounds, don't change your ad if you don't need to. Each time you change your ad Facebook will reapprove it and launch it with Facebook's most up to date algorithms which in the end serve Facebook over you.

I have tested thousands of individual variables and I have a tremendous amount of institutional memory, but I never become complacent because Facebook is always changing.

About James

James Dicks has spent more than 25 years building business through marketing practices and experience only garnered through real world application. James is a McGraw-Hill International best-selling author and has been seen on all major affiliates around the country including ABC, NBC, CBS, FOX, and CNBC.

As a consultant/contractor and owner operator, James' forte is in marketing and creating brand awareness. As an entrepreneur, James has managed all aspects of business growth – from working with nearly a thousand people to running a business with more than 150 employees.

James is a strong believer in the longevity of a customer. It's not just customer acquisition, but customer loyalty creates winning combinations that will ultimately prove positive for the company's bottom line growth.

James brings his technology background to DNA Pulse where he serves as CEO. He specializes in "out-of-the-box" thinking to successfully integrate the latest technology with business sales and marketing goals. James specializes in using this technology, background and experience to help businesses bridge the gap of traditional advertising and social media advertising. To do this, DNA Pulse focuses its core competencies on new media technologies – such as mobile media advertising and marketing, as well as near horizon media opportunities such as location-based advertising.

James is a member of a national information technology subcommittee for an office of the Department of Defense, where he collaborates with other technology industry leaders that collectively foster technology advancements and integration.

As both a former Marine and dedicated family man, James strives to make a positive difference in the lives of every person he meets.

CHAPTER 10

PEOPLE OF IMPACT: MASTERING SUCCESS BY ASSOCIATION

BY JW DICKS & NICK NANTON

Oprah was very confused.

It was 1996 and the queen of daytime TV was used to having the last word in any debate. She was perceived as the voice of truth by her adoring fans and was lucky enough to avoid any serious backlash to whatever words of wisdom she proclaimed during her daily top-rated one-hour talk show.

Then, one day, she and a guest began discussing the recent mad cow disease scare in Great Britain, an epidemic that had forced the slaughter of over four million cattle. Mad cow had just begun to crop up in Canada and Oprah wondered aloud if beef was still safe to eat in the U.S.A.

And that's when the beef industry pushed back. Big time.

Under a Texas law, one company sued Oprah for libel, claiming her comments caused cattle futures to drop 10 percent the day after the episode, and beef prices to fall from 62 cents to 55 cents per pound. They filed for damages of over $12 million – money Oprah was on the hook for if she lost the case. And suddenly, her main weapon – her voice – was taken away from her, because she wasn't allowed to discuss the matter while the case was being litigated.

That's when Phil McGraw came into her life.

McGraw had been a psychologist who had been offering motivational seminars designed to help people get out of their emotional boxes. Although the seminars became successful in parts of Texas, McGraw didn't see how he could expand much further beyond the state – so he cashed out of the company. Instead, McGraw co-founded the company Courtroom Sciences to help legal teams coach witnesses and select juries. His ability to quickly read people brought him a lot of success in this arena – and also brought him Oprah.

Oprah's team hired McGraw and soon, he was instructing the daytime talk-show queen in how to frame her remarks in the most effective way when she was on the stand, so she could deliver the right message to the jury.

And he saw an opportunity.

He made it a point to ingratiate himself with Oprah, offering tons of his downhome wisdom in his Texas drawl, until Winfrey couldn't help but love the way this man held her attention, and how effectively he communicated with everyone around her. Most of all, she loved the way he made her feel okay about what was going on, how he helped her understand she had done nothing wrong and that she just had to stand her ground to get through this.

She did. And she put McGraw on her show several times – and each time, he caused a sensation. Which is why her production company decided to give Dr. Phil his own daily hour-long show, which was an immediate success.

Dr. Phil McGraw, or Dr. Phil, as he is now known to the masses, had finally found a way to become the MediaMaster he always wanted to be. All it took was gaining access to the audience of the biggest MediaMaster in the world – Oprah.

Of course, Dr. Phil wasn't the only one to create a lucrative career through Oprah's endorsement. Dr. Oz, as well as a host of other authors, fitness and diet gurus and other experts all found new levels of success through exposure to Oprah's audience. But all of these professionals were ready for their moment in the sun. They had crafted their message and prepared themselves for the spotlight – otherwise they wouldn't have impressed Oprah to begin with.

Now – how about you?

In this excerpt from our upcoming book, Impact, we're going to share another strategy to achieving success as a MediaMaster—a thought leader or expert in your industry who knows how to quickly uncover and tap into a receptive target market. More specifically, we're going to discuss the people who can deliver people – those, like Oprah Winfrey, who already have a built-in following that could form the bedrock of your MediaMaster platform.

THE CHAMPIONS OF YOUR CORE AUDIENCE

You most likely already know who is the best audience for your message. That audience could be made up of, depending on your expertise, anyone from entrepreneurs to people desperate to lose weight. Identifying who they are is the easy part. Getting them to invest time and energy into actually listening to you, however, is the hard part.

That's why your next step should be identifying people they *already* listen to – and developing a relationship with them.

Just as Dr. Phil found his audience through Oprah, you too can gain access to a built-in following by finding a way to connect with the "champions" of your intended audience – the people they know and trust – and getting them on board to be your advocate with their group.

Let's talk about three ways to get that done, and showcase each method's main advantage and disadvantage.

I. Mentorship

Jim Rohn was an Idaho farm boy and Sears clerk who became an incredibly successful MediaMaster at a young age. His career as a motivational speaker and author made him a millionaire by age 31 – and, about 20 years later, his message attracted a 17-year-old boy looking for some direction in life; his name was Tony Robbins and Rohn quickly became his mentor.

Like Robbins, many of the great MediaMasters learned their craft and found their audience by allowing themselves to be mentored by other established MediaMasters. That's how the two of us, the authors of this chapter, started working together, in a mentor-mentee relationship. Of course, that's an easy step to take if you're 17 years old; it's either that or behind a McDonalds counter for most teens. If you're a lawyer, doctor or other established professional, however, you may feel you're beyond the stage in life where you need anyone to mentor you.

But keep in mind *you are crossing over into a new field*. Whereas you may be very accomplished in your specific profession, you are new to the world of MediaMastery – and allowing someone who's successful in that world to mentor you can give you invaluable access to their expertise and their audience as well.

Being mentored doesn't mean you have to work in their office and fetch them coffee. It means you can build a relationship in which they show you the ropes and you provide value on your side. You can pay them for their time or provide services through your expertise. There are a lot of creative ways you can make it work and we still approach people to mentor us on different areas of our lives and business, it's just a smart thing to do!

Whatever your field might be, remember how much you *didn't* know at the start, before you gained the experience and knowledge necessary to excel in it. You learned from others who *did* have that experience and knowledge, because you knew they had the goods and you didn't as of yet. Well, this situation is no different. You may be, for example, the most acclaimed psychologist in the world – but translating that skill to MediaMastery is trickier than you might think.

And remember, in the end, if the MediaMaster likes what you're doing and how you're doing it, he or she will not be shy about giving you exposure to their audience. Part of their value to their following is bringing new people to their attention, people who have worthwhile content and messages to share.

So, open yourself up to the idea of a MediaMaster mentor. Many of the greats began that way and that approach paid off for them a million times over.

Just ask Tony Robbins.

Mentoring Advantage: *You gain first-hand knowledge from an experienced MediaMaster and access to his/her (hopefully!) large audience.*

Mentoring Disadvantage: *In many cases you can end up tethered to a single individual, which could limit your ultimate opportunities – and your fortunes could rise and fall with that individual as well.*

II. Networking

If you're more the independent sort, networking can be a way to get what you want in terms of tapping into a vibrant and receptive audience. Networking, however, can be time-consuming and you will, for the most part, have to provide your own direction, because you'll be completely in charge of the process with no one to really give you an overall plan of attack.

With networking, your objective will be to connect with *influencers* in your particular target group – the kind of folks others in your audience listen to and respect. Instead of focusing on one particular individual, you'll want to form relationships with many different influencers and hope that they use their standing in the community to promote your thoughts and ideas. This can be done both through virtual social networks (such as Facebook and Twitter), real-life networks (such as conventions, events, joining organizations, etc.) or, most effectively, a combination of both.

Suppose you're a plastic surgeon who wants to be the go-to person on how to improve someone's appearance. On social media, you would want to "follow" every account (magazines, organizations, other leading doctors) that deals with that subject matter. You'll then want to engage them on the topic when it comes up on their social media – by supporting them, commenting, sharing their news and offering them some sort of benefit with your presence. You would also want to try and attend conventions and gatherings that focus on your subject matter, and personally sit down with the leaders and speakers you encounter there. In today's virtual world, face-to-face meetings are becoming increasingly rare – and, as a result, increasingly effective!

These influencers are the kinds of contacts that are invaluable when you begin distributing your MediaMaster content, such as podcasts, books, videos, or whatever you put out there in order to build your following. If you've been generous with these influencers, then they're going to be generous with you in terms of sharing your content with their followers. We have met many of the people we work with to this day through events. Richard Branson, Steve Forbes, Brian Tracy, Jack Canfield, Dr. Peter Diamandis, Dan Kennedy, Dr. Nido Qubein, Dan Sullivan and Joe Polish come to mind as just a few of them—all whom we have gone on to work with in some capacity.

Networking Advantage: *You will reach a wider pool of potential followers, because you'll be connecting with a variety of influencers in different locations.*

Networking Disadvantage: *This will take much more time and effort than simply hooking up with one MediaMaster and working exclusively with them.*

III. Advocate Marketing

Advocate Marketing puts together the best attributes of networking and mentorship to create a powerful group of "brand advocates" who have the ability to further your MediaMastery in a significant way. It involves reaching out to the rich and powerful that are a vital part of the field in which you want to make your impact - and creating relationships with them that combine the best elements of mentoring and networking.

Our friend, Sean Stephenson, for example, is a very successful MediaMaster who employs this method to this day. He has twenty-two people in his advocate network who are well-connected in different industries. Some of them have gravitated to him on their own because they believe in his message. With others, he has had to work hard to find ways to gain access to them. In all cases, these are powerful people who will still accept his call when he reaches out to them – and will help him out with a simple request if he asks.

In return, he sees himself as "on call" for these people 24/7 if they want something from him. For instance, since he is a licensed psychologist, he will help out with an emergency with, say, a relative, if needed. He also will "trickle value" on these people throughout the year. As an example, he might read a book that has a lot of thoughts or hard information that he knows one of his advocates would find useful. So he will send that advocate a copy of the book through "snail mail," along with a note that distills the most useful portions from the book for them to skim (these are busy people, after all!). It all comes down to what Tony Robbins called his most important advice from his mentor Jim Rohn: The secret to life is to *find a way to do more for others than anyone else is doing*. We call it "the value equation."

Advocate Marketing, however, works best for those who have already established some level of MediaMastery. You have to have some kind of reputation already in place, either as a MediaMaster or in your chosen profession, to get close to these kinds of "people in high places" and be seen as useful to them. And you will have to spend a lot of time and effort in marketing to your advocates in order to maintain the relationships. If you are successful in creating a strong Advocate Network, however, you've created a huge resource that will definitely boost your profile in a myriad of different ways.

Advocate Marketing Advantage: *You create a group of powerful boosters who have the ability to connect you with a wider audience as well as other powerful backers.*

Advocate Marketing Disadvantage: *The Catch-22 is you have to have some power in order to connect with the powerful. This is a difficult proposition unless you have a high profile already in your profession or have experienced some MediaMaster success.*

To sum up, whether you choose mentorship, networking or advocate marketing will likely depend on how advanced a MediaMaster you currently are.

If you're just a **beginner**, think about finding a mentor to help you learn. And remember mentors are always proud of their pupils, so they're very likely to present you to their public.

If you're already fairly **active, networking** might be the best path for you, particularly if you are generating content on a regular basis and doing social media in the role of MediaMaster.

If you've **developed a reputation** – or are already a **fairly high-profile** individual within your profession – consider **Advocate Marketing**. You will have more to offer truly influential people if they see you as someone helpful to them.

CONNECTING WITH PEOPLE OF IMPACT

How do you identify and hook up with a Person of Impact, someone with stature and/or influence in the community you want to reach? How do you get them to pay attention to your messaging – and share it with their own followers? Read the following "Action Steps" and you'll find the answers you want! .

■**Action Step #1: Identify your targets.**

Begin this Action Guide by either identifying MediaMasters you might want for a mentor, or a number of influencers or Advocates you want to network with. If you're not sure about who your People of Impact should be, it's time to do some research!

■**Action Step #2: Offer to help.**

Influencers are in a position where they constantly need to come up with new content and new viewpoints to stay relevant to their community. By providing this kind of quality material to them on a regular basis, you become useful to them – and they begin to rely on you to help out. This is really easy to accomplish if you have an area of expertise that's relevant to this community – so you can become the "go-to" guy or gal on that subject matter.

With that in mind, consider what you have to offer these People of Impact that will make an impact on them.

■Action Step #3: Create a conversation

Are you knowledgeable? Interesting? Even funny on occasions? Then make it a point to start conversations in the community you're aiming at on Facebook, Twitter, Pinterest, or whatever social site where your target group is active. Ask a question, ask for feedback, share a news item, do whatever it takes to interest people in your posts and begin dialogues with them, so that you become an active presence. And by all means, be sure and comment on others' posts – while making sure to stay positive, respectful and, yes, polite in your interactions. We all know the kind of noise that can erupt on the Internet at any given moment – just make sure you're part of the solution, not the problem!

■Action Step #4: Add Value

Let's repeat Jim Rohn's number one piece of advice to Tony Robbins: The secret to life is to *find a way to do more for others than anyone else is doing*. There is no question that this is the most effective approach to this kind of networking. The more you can be of use to People of Impact, the more they will promote you, share your content and, in general, give you your "props." Sharing interesting content, useful advice, free services in your area of expertise and so forth are all ways to bring that value to their table – and make them a fan of *you*, rather than just vice-versa. Look for ways to make a positive difference in their lives – just like Dr. Phil did for Oprah – and they'll hopefully do the same for you.

■Action Step #5: Co-create content.

It's always a major coup when you can somehow attach your name to someone who's a huge celebrity. This is why we hook up our clients with such major MediaMasters as Jack Canfield,

Brian Tracy and Peter Diamandis. We put our people in books headlined by them, in television interviews with them, and even in person—standing side-by-side at our special events throughout the year. When you're seen in a collaborative effort with a Person of Impact, you share in their reflected glory.

With influencers of lesser stature, there are a number of ways you can put this tactic into action. You can "guest blog" on their site, for example, do a podcast with them or make them a part of any other form of content you can easily share online. One of the keys to this is to associate yourself with those with a larger platform than yours in the field you are trying to get known in, so you can continually rise in people's perceptions of your standing in the community.

Identifying and building bonds with people who can deliver their audiences to you is one of the most important steps on your MediaMaster journey. When you can translate some of the public's trust in them to your side, you've jumped over a significant hurdle that will undoubtedly aid the perception of your standing in the community. You can't be a MediaMaster without an audience – so connect with influencers who already have one in place. It's the fastest way to build your own following for years to come.

About Jack

JW Dicks, Esq., is a Wall Street Journal Best-Selling Author®, two-time Emmy Award-Winning Executive Producer, XPrize board member, and co-founder of The National Academy of Best-Selling Authors® and The National Association of Experts, Writers and Speakers®.

JW is the CEO of DNAgency and is a strategic business development consultant to both domestic and international clients. He has been quoted on business and financial topics in national media such as *USA Today, The Wall Street Journal, Newsweek, Forbes, CNBC.com, Fortune Magazine* and *Success Magazine.*

Considered a ThoughtLeader® and curator of information, JW has more than forty-three published business and legal books to his credit and has co-authored with legends like Brian Tracy, Jack Canfield, Tom Hopkins, Dr. Nido Qubein, Dr. Ivan Misner, Dan Kennedy, and Mari Smith. He is the Editor and Publisher of *ThoughtLeader® Magazine.*

JW is called the "Expert to the Experts" and has appeared on business television shows airing on ABC, NBC, CBS, and FOX affiliates around the country and co-produces and syndicates a line of franchised business television shows such as *Success Today, Wall Street Today, Hollywood Live, Washington Connection,* and *Profiles of Success.*

JW and his wife of forty-five years, Linda, have two daughters, four granddaughters, and two Yorkies. He is a sixth-generation Floridian and splits his time between his home in Orlando and his beach house on Florida's west coast.

About Nick

An Emmy Award-Winning Director and Producer, Nick Nanton, Esq., produces media and branded content for top thought leaders and media personalities around the world. Recognized as a leading expert on branding and storytelling, Nick has authored more than two dozen Best-Selling books (including *The Wall Street Journal* Best-Seller, *StorySelling*™) and produced and directed more than 40 documentaries, earning 5 Emmy Awards and 14 nominations. Nick speaks to audiences internationally on the topics of branding, entertainment, media, business and storytelling at major universities and events.

As the CEO of DNA Media, Nick oversees a portfolio of companies including: The Dicks + Nanton Agency (an international agency with more than 3000 clients in 36 countries), Dicks + Nanton Productions, Ambitious.com, CelebrityPress, DNA Films®, DNA Pulse, and DNA Capital Ventures. Nick is an award-winning director, producer and songwriter who has worked on everything from large-scale events to television shows with the likes of Steve Forbes, Ivanka Trump, Sir Richard Branson, Rudy Ruettiger (inspiration for the Hollywood blockbuster, *RUDY*), Jack Canfield (*The Secret*, creator of the *Chicken Soup for the Soul* Series), Brian Tracy, Michael E. Gerber, Tom Hopkins, Dan Kennedy and many more.

Nick has been seen in *USA Today*, *The Wall Street Journal*, *Newsweek*, *BusinessWeek*, *Inc. Magazine*, *The New York Times*, *Entrepreneur® Magazine*, *Forbes*, and *FastCompany*. He has appeared on ABC, NBC, CBS, and FOX television affiliates across the country as well as on CNN, FOX News, CNBC, and MSNBC from coast to coast.

Nick is a member of the Florida Bar, a voting member of The National Academy of Recording Arts & Sciences (Home to the GRAMMYs), a member of The National Academy of Television Arts & Sciences (Home to the EMMYs), Co-founder of The National Academy of Best-Selling Authors®, and serves on the Innovation Board of the XPRIZE Foundation, a non-profit organization dedicated to bringing about "radical breakthroughs for the benefit of humanity" through incentivized competition – best known for its Ansari XPRIZE which incentivized the first private space flight and was the catalyst for Richard Branson's Virgin Galactic. Nick also enjoys serving as an

Elder at Orangewood Church, working with Young Life, Downtown Credo Orlando, Entrepreneurs International and rooting for the Florida Gators with his wife Kristina and their three children, Brock, Bowen and Addison.

Learn more at:
- www.NickNanton.com
- www.CelebrityBrandingAgency.com

CHAPTER 11

THE PERILS OF PAYMENTS: FOUR STRATEGIES TO AVOID MERCHANT ACCOUNT COLLAPSE

BY MIKE DORLAND

I take VISA, MasterCard and American Express. I'm the only homeless guy in America who can take a credit card.
~ Abe Hagenston

Debit or Credit?

I'd like to tell you a very enterprising story about a man named "Honest Abe." No, I'm not referring to the 16th President of the United States. This story is about Abe Hagenston, . . . homeless Abe Hagenston.

It was January of 2016. I was spending time in Detroit where I was fortunate enough to work on the Emmy-Nominated PBS TV show, *Start Up*. The host, Gary Bredow, travels around the country interviewing small business owners to hear their personal stories, and to find out what it really takes to start a successful business from the ground up.

Gary and I were headed from his multi-media production studio to a great local eatery for lunch in Detroit's Corktown district. That's when I first heard about Abe.

Gary is no stranger to finding interesting stories of achievement from entrepreneurial-minded people. This story was a little different, though. He explained how he had heard a local radio report about a homeless man who was accepting credit card payments as he solicited money at busy intersections in Detroit.

Abe and his vagrant friends had banded together like a union of sorts. Each of them would work different area "hot spots" for pan handling. At the end of each day, they would come together and split the proceeds evenly. While they were all successful in bringing money back to the group, they kept hearing the same common objection. "Sorry! I don't have any cash on me!"

Abe originally started collecting money to help replace his broken prescription glasses. He soon found he was collecting enough money to get himself fed for the day, but he would never make enough money to replace his glasses at the rate he was going. That's when the idea hit him. They might not have cash, but they MUST have a credit card!

Abe was right. His ingenuity and awareness of technology enabled him to connect a card reader to his smartphone and collect payments from those that would help. Abe and his friends saw an immediate increase in collections. Whether it was the novelty of it or his charismatic approach, the people were ready to pay.

As many successful entrepreneurs do, Abe then looked to expand his business. He created a website to collect donations and allow people to book him and his friends for odd jobs around their home or business. He wasn't done there, though.

His next enterprising idea was to create websites for people and businesses to promote their product or service. Once he was able to get a few of these jobs, he realized he could help teach other homeless people to do the same. His goals were lofty as he wanted to help a new homeless person become a millionaire every day.

Entrepreneurs need to know this!

I wish I could tell you that's how Abe's story worked out but, unfortunately, there's no happy ending here. The last we knew, Abe was still collecting money on his favorite street corners and his website advertising his services for hire was no longer active. There are, however, some important takeaways that anyone looking to be successful in their business can learn.

If Abe stuck to the tried and true methods of spanging (pronounced "spain-jing"), he'd be carrying around a coffee can full of coins. You and I may not give Abe our cards for payment or hire him to build a website no matter how "honest" he is, but some people will. That is a point many people who are undecided about starting a business or are still relatively new in their entrepreneurial path miss.

Whatever product or service you are offering, you and your business have a distinct voice. With that will come your own unique set of customers that want to hear it. It is you and your personal experience that crafts your message. Your message will resonate differently with different people. The successful business owners realize they can't appeal to everyone, so they focus on the people that resonate with their message or brand. That's what Abe was able to do.

The other takeaway from Abe is that *once you craft your message and find your audience, you need to be ready to take their money!* There is nothing more exciting than making a sale when your product or service solved your customer's problem. That's why you do what you do. But you also need to be ready to take their payment when the exchange of your goods and services are complete.

In my story, we see that Abe quickly figured out that credit and debit cards are the preferred method of payment. In fact, I challenge you to find someone under the age of 35 who still carries cash with them. Those days are long gone.

With the increasing technology available through social media and various platforms, many people want to share their product, service or message through information products they sell online. It is the fastest most effective way to reach the people that want to hear your unique message.

You've seen the ads on Facebook. The "Suggested Post" with a product or service offer in your timeline. This is no accident. The person running that ad thinks their product or service is something you can use or would be interested in.

Maybe you are looking to lose weight and see a catchy post that looks like you might be interested. You follow the link, read the information and decide you want to buy their program. Next, you enter your credit card information into the form and just like that you know how to lose 10 pounds in 10 days because they emailed their product to you instantly!

Here's the secret most people don't know, though.

The person that made that sale and anyone else who sells their products or service this way is considered "high risk" by the merchant service providers.

(The merchant service provider is the third party that business owners contract with to accept your credit card payment.)

It isn't a bad thing to be considered "high risk," but it is how these providers see you. The fact is, our homeless friend Abe is less of a risk to the merchant provider than you would be selling your product or service online! Doesn't seem right, does it?

Any time your card is not present to be swiped the merchant service provider sees this as a higher risk of fraud. If someone uses a fraudulent card to buy a product or a consumer is unhappy with the product they purchased, the cardholder issues a chargeback.

When a chargeback happens, the issuing bank takes the disputed money from the merchant service provider. The provider then takes the money from the business owner until the dispute is resolved. If the business owner does not have the money to cover the dispute the provider is stuck paying the cardholder back. This is what creates the risk for the provider and why this kind of business is considered "high risk."

Imagine you create a compelling offer for $97 and sell it to 1000 people. That would generate a gross sales amount of $97,000! Feels great, doesn't it? Except what if 5 of those people, or 0.5% of your total sales, decided to dispute the transaction and issue a chargeback? Not only will the merchant provider take the money back for the 5 chargebacks, they will freeze your account and hold ALL your money not deposited until the disputes are cleared up. That could be 30 days or more of not receiving your money! ... all $97,000 of it!

Can you imagine the anger and frustration of working hard to create something of value for your customer, getting paid from a sale and having your merchant provider hold your money and not give it to you? **Sadly, this happens every day to well-intentioned business owners.** They did everything right except choose the right merchant service provider.

Now you know why this kind of business is considered "high risk" and what can happen if your chargeback ratio exceeds your merchant provider's limits. Here's what you can do to help you identify the right merchant service provider for you.

I want to give you **Four Simple Steps** to take to help you navigate through the setup of your "high risk" merchant account:

#1. Get Solid Underwriting

Solid underwriting doesn't mean that you can't get an account setup quickly, but the RIGHT companies aren't going to set you up in record speed. The biggest trick to having a stable merchant account is finding the provider who REALLY knows your business AND really wants it. If they do their due diligence on the front end and really understand your business, they won't have a reason to close your merchant account.

If you feel like the underwriter or your merchant provider representative is trying to understand your business model, you're moving in the right direction. If you're asked for the minimum pieces of information below, you'll know you're working with a company that is less likely to shut down your account:

- Personal info (Address, Birthday, SSN) – required on all merchant accounts
- Business Info (EIN, Articles of Incorporation, Voided Check) – required on all merchant accounts.
- Business Model Info (this is the one low-risk providers skip)
  - How are taking orders (swiped, key entered or online and WHERE)
  - How are you delivering your product? Digital delivery, UPS, live events, etc.
  - How do you create your own product or repurpose someone else's?
  - How long after the sale is the product delivered?
  - What is your guarantee?
  - Do you have any recurring payments?
- Access to your product/logins for your membership site.

Good high-risk providers want to understand your business model! You don't want to have your account shut down, frozen or suspended. Solid underwriting $\equiv$ No shutting down accounts $\equiv$ Happy Entrepreneur.

#2. Setup Multiple Accounts with Different Member Banks

You want to diversify your merchant account volume across multiple merchant accounts. Why?

Two reasons:

1. If one merchant account gets shut down, you have others up and running.
2. If one merchant account provider holds your money, they won't have ALL your money.

But here's the catch! Each merchant account provider is tied to what's called a "member bank." The member bank is the entity that is directly tied to Visa, MasterCard, Discover and American Express. These are also referred to as "the associations."

If you have three merchant accounts that all have the same member bank, when one is closed they are all likely to be closed.

The setup of this can be tricky. You really want to work with someone that understands the industry. That's the best approach because the curve is steep here.

The good news is that brokers in the industry are all paid on the back end, so you're never paying any more to work with a broker (with the good ones), but you get their expertise. The bad news is there are very few good brokers in this space.

#3. Use Load Balancing

You can have multiple accounts with multiple member banks, but you can't just use one account and keep the others around "just in case." If an account is dormant for more than a few months many providers will automatically close the account due to inactivity.

Beyond that, you don't have the same protection. If all your sales go through one account and the merchant account provider decides to hold your money, or a portion of it, you won't be receiving any of the money from your sales!

You want to distribute your sales across multiple merchant accounts automatically. It doesn't have to be distributed evenly, the goal is simply to have it happening in the background without you having to manage it.

There are only a few companies that allow some form of rotating through merchant accounts, but only one has a patent-pending feature called "Load Balancing." It was designed to address the challenge "high risk" business owners have: keeping money in their own bank accounts instead of their processors.

#4. "Season" Accounts

The longer you have an account, with a good processor, the more stable your account is. Underwriters put more weight on your history than any other single thing.

What really terrifies underwriters are large spikes in sales volume on a new account. Again, if you're working with the right provider, the likelihood of an issue decreases dramatically. Even if you have a history with a provider, it's never ideal to take an account from zero to a million in a month.

The key is to add volume to several merchant accounts instead of one and increase it over time.

For example, if you're a new company and you think you're going to process $100,000 your first month; instead of setting up one account with a $100,000 limit, you should setup three accounts and put $33,000 through each of them. Going from zero to $33,000 is not as big a deal as zero to $100,000. You're effectively cutting the merchant account provider's liability down to only 33% of what it would have been. This is a win-win for you and the merchant provider.

Your goal here is to create some sort of stable growth on your accounts for several months in a row. Obviously, every business model is different, but that's your goal. Once your accounts have been up and running for several months or years, your merchant account providers will be much less sensitive to any kind of change in your account whether it be a spike in volume, a new product offering, a new marketing model or an increase in chargebacks.

The world of merchant accounts can seem like a minefield for "high risk" business owners. If you haven't had that experience yet, I'm sure you know people that have. There is far more information that I could share outside of these four steps to navigating the merchant account setup process, but I know the hardest part in any business is going from concept to revenue. Setting up your merchant account is a vital step to making this happen.

The good news is you're not alone! A new report from Forrester Research Inc. predicts online sales in the United States are expected to reach $523 billion in the next five years, up 56% from $335 billion in 2015.

There's never been a better time to become successful by sharing your message, product or service online. There are people ready to learn about what you have to offer and more importantly they are ready to PAY for it! Just be sure you've found the right merchant service provider before they do.

About Mike

Mike Dorland helps simplify the connections that make commerce possible for entrepreneurs and their customers.

Mike began his career in business by working his way up the ranks of a family-owned paint company in Lansing, Michigan. At the age of 26, he was managing production, distribution, retail and commercial sales channels for this regional paint manufacturer.

With this experience and knowledge, Mike decided to help other businesses succeed as he began working for the largest state retail trade association in the nation. There he worked to provide revenue-producing solutions and reduce the overall costs of their members' bottom line.

It was during this time that Mike began to focus on the payments industry and how businesses could leverage technology to accept payments from their customers.

By the end of 2012, Mike had risen through the ranks of the payments industry as he became one of the first Electronic Transactions Association Certified Payments Professionals (ETA CPP) in the country. The ETA CPP program sets the standard for professional performance in the payments industry and is a symbol of excellence.

From there, Mike continued his journey to the top of the payments industry by accepting a position with the global leader in payments, First Data. There he began working with businesses from all industries in their Mid-Market segment. He was responsible for managing key client relationships and identified products and solutions to fit the client's needs.

After two successful years in the Mid-Market segment, Mike was promoted to the National segment where he now manages the largest and most influential clients in the First Data portfolio. He specializes in Alternative Markets, Ecommerce, Casino & Gaming, Money Transfer Services, Hotel, Travel and Airlines.

In addition to his work in the payments industry, Mike has also served as the

Corporate Communications Director for the Emmy-Nominated PBS TV Show, *Start Up*. In this role, he supported the Host and Creator, Gary Bredow, and Executive Producer, Jenny Feterovich, as they worked together to secure corporate sponsorships for the show.

Outside of his love for entrepreneurs, Mike is committed to raising awareness for the prevention of HIV and AIDS in Zambia and the developing world. He proudly supports The Muchimba Music Foundation where he serves as an Awareness Ambassador.

Mike's friend and co-founder, Thomas Muchimba Buttenschøn, has spread his messages of positivity and hope through his pervasive and powerful music. The Muchimba Music Foundation harnesses that power and uses music to enlighten, to empower and to draw people together.

You can connect with Mike at:

- www.mikedorland.com
- www.linkedin.com/in/mike-dorland

You can connect with *Start Up* TV Show at:

- www.startup-usa.com

You can learn about Thomas's amazing story and connect with the Muchimba Music Foundation at:

- www.doinmydrugs.com
- www.muchimba.org

CHAPTER 12

GOING GLOBAL WITH YOUR COMPANY
TOP SEVEN SECRETS FOR EXPANDING TO OTHER COUNTRIES

BY DR. ALBERT ALLEN

What is more important – knowledge or action? Action of course, because if you had all the knowledge in the world and you don't act, it is as if you had no knowledge at all.
~ Alexandra Allen

Why Do I Take Companies Overseas?

Why do I do what I do? I believe that people from all countries should have access to superior goods and services we take for granted in the U.S., and that innovators should expand their reach internationally. I grew up seeing the positive effects for companies of going global, as well as for people worldwide. That is why I take companies international. When I was a toddler, my Diplomat father took our family to live in Latin America, Asia and later Europe, where I learned cultures, business methods, history and languages, and made valuable contacts I use in business to take companies global, build modern real estate, as well as to bring technology and innovations to help modernize countries. For centuries, family members were ship owners doing business globally, and I heard stories from my grandmother that captivated me. I returned overseas after an MBA and DBA to invest with companies, do business, bring help and lived in Latin America, Asia, Europe and the Middle East, bringing companies and organizations into new countries. I do this because I have been part of companies that are highly profitable overseas, that bring lasting improvement to people worldwide as doors open and opportunities emerge.

INTRODUCTION

In Going Global, Doors Open and Opportunities Emerge

Luck is preparation meeting opportunity.
~ Oprah Winfrey

There will be more companies, organizations and services going global than ever before in history, making owners incredible fortunes and influential, changing lives of millions worldwide for the better. Maybe you work at a large corporation, a brick-and-mortar company, a tech services operation, a virtual help outsource, a mid-sized mom-and-pop shop, a franchise, a non-profit or ministry, and you have thought about going international into other countries. Most probably the complexity of where to start, what to do or the high cost of setting up operations, has prevented you.

But what if I shared with you a low-cost fail-proof and quick way to expand overseas – using partner strategies developed from years of experience taking several dozen companies international. You don't have to build a sales force. There is one already built for you that has the customers you need. You don't have to get permits, get government permissions, sign leases, get utilities, do all those things to go into business in another country. All you need to do is to <u>focus on finding the right partners and training them</u>. Easier said than done, right?

Going global is the stuff fortunes are made from, because you can leverage what you have already developed and then leverage it again, using partners to grow exponentially instead of geometrically. Oftentimes, overseas you will find less advanced competition, you can have the advantage of being first-to-market, you could be the innovator and disruptive force able to capture low-hanging high-profit customers. With partner strategies, you can leverage other peoples' time, other peoples' money, other peoples' specific market knowledge, other peoples' market contacts, other peoples' ideas, other peoples' work, and other peoples' solutions. Going global with your organization using local partner strategies offers incredible profit opportunities, sales expansion and the potential to capture growing markets – opening doors of opportunity.

Quickly, do research on what percentage of sales and growth come from overseas for all different types and sizes of companies – from single operations to McDonald's, Microsoft, Bechtel, call centers, Facebook, technology-related operations, Compassion International, manufacturing and other companies, organizations, services, industries or non-profits – to realize the potential. Then, research where the current growth potential is now, and where the growth in the future will be. The potential is staggering. It is profitable, rewarding and a lot easier than you ever imagined to grow internationally, but it requires action and focus.

Based on what I have learned after working over 25 years with some of the most experienced professionals helping companies enter new countries, here are seven top secrets to expand globally into new countries.

1) Be clear about who your ideal customers are, and what differentiates you as a company.

Know Thyself.
~ The Oracle at Delphi

The first step is introspection, and you need to know the exact profiles of your best customers, because this is where your sales and profit will come from. You need to partner with companies that have years of established relationships with these customers and have access to what you are looking for. You need to plug into the networks that have taken years of effort and money to develop, and these networks of established relationships are what you will leverage to make profitable sales. Michael Porter says that loyalty of a customer is more important than satisfaction of a customer, and developing loyalty takes years of doing business and relationship to build.

You also need to think through your USP or unique selling proposition. What is it that differentiates your company and makes you unique to others? This differentiation needs to be positioned correctly given the culture and the way business is conducted in that country, so that it has value for the customer. For example, McDonalds in many developing countries, is a restaurant for social gathering as opposed to fast food. What makes you different? . . . Is it speed, quality, low-cost, made-to-order, or a specialized way of doing business? To succeed long term in business, you need an SCA or Sustainable Competitive Advantage that makes you different. What makes you different from your competitors? Once you are clear about this, you can begin to focus outwardly.

2) Be referred by top people to influential local partners who are working with customers you want.

The purpose of a business is to find, get, keep, and to take care of customers in a cost-effective manner in order to turn a profit.
~ Michael Porter

It is all about the customer, and business people from countries overseas are different and may have different ways of doing business with customers. For example, in the United States, someone from New York City is different to someone from Iowa, Texas, or Los Angeles. This difference is even more marked when it comes to doing business from one country to another overseas, or from regions inside a country. A businessman in Mexico City handles partners and business customers differently than a businessman in Beijing, Toronto, Frankfurt, London, Hong Kong, Sao Paulo, Paris, Singapore or Taiwan.

In general, businessmen overseas place a high value on personal relationships in business, and on levels of trust in those relationships. Established business friendships are important components of conducting business overseas. This is why being referred by someone who is held in high regard transfers trust and a stamp of approval. If done correctly, it reduces years of effort, presence and goodwill. There is no substitute for this overseas.

3) At first, focus on finding and developing many options.

Your most unhappy customers are your
greatest source of learning.
~ Bill Gates

Finding the correct partner is a process and all about fit. There has to be the correct fit between you and your potential partner. That is why you need to make sure that you develop many options that could work as partners. Remember, in most negotiations, the side that has most options is in a better position.

Mentally, you need to put yourself in the mindset initially that you are not looking for partners, but that you are developing as many good options as you can from which you will later analyze and prioritize. Do not rush this process, and leave no stone unturned. You need to ask a lot of questions and gather information that may help in making a decision.

Clarity is a key to success. You need to be very clear what you are looking for, and just as clear in expressing to others what is needed. Clearly, tell those you are talking to the skill set that is needed, what you are looking for, what is expected and how success is measured. Things that are not quantified and measured with specifics, do not get done.

4) Don't impose a United States way of thinking overseas in business relationships.

It is not the strongest that survive, nor the most intelligent,
but the one most responsive to change.
~ Charles Darwin

In the U.S. in general, efficiency, time, and money are important. In other countries, these can be less important than the proper time for face-to-face relationships and high levels of control. Overseas companies and organizations tend to be more hierarchical where bosses make most major decisions. In part because of culture, history and the way the countries were colonized, there is little discretionary control in middle and senior management. It is mostly the owners that decide important questions. This makes decisions move slower and become cumbersome. Remember that efficiency and time are not always the main issue overseas, but control.

Because trust is so important in doing business overseas, developing trust needs to be given the proper amount of time and attention to develop. Trust is built with others through having shared experiences, knowing the same people, sharing past performance together and a bond of personal friendship that can be called on when needed. Knowing the right people and having them know you is important to success in business overseas.

5) Analyze pros and cons of partner options by using a ranking system.

Business has to be involving, it has to be fun, and it has
to exercise your creative instincts.
~ Richard Branson

Analyzing options can take many forms, but in the end, you need to lay out in order of importance, strengths and weaknesses of options to compare and contrast. This involves ranking strengths and weaknesses in order of importance to you, and weighing these in order of how they affect achieving your results.

There are many things you are looking for in partners too long to list here, but among the important considerations are:

- Can he deliver what you need?
- Will he follow according to your specifications?
- Is he easy to get along with and is there a "fit"?
- Is he financially capable of carrying out his part?
- Is he interested in your processes and is this important to him?
- Does he have the correct people in place to follow through?
- Can he ramp up effectively?

Future potential is a factor that oftentimes is not considered correctly. I have seen companies fail time and time again. You want to be able to grow your relationships, so you want to look for growth potential. Remember that Michael Jordan was once on a fifth grade basketball team, and it is in your ability to recognize future potential and growth that you will be successful.

6) Enter a country with two or three partners.

The first one gets the oyster; the second gets the shell.
~ Andrew Carnegie

It takes time and effort to train partners and get operations going, so it is better to have several options at a time. What if the partner you chose has problems that he can't solve or he doesn't deliver what he promised? Having several partners in the country makes good business sense to assure success. So, set up a system where you can enter a country with several partners at a time.

The truth is you don't really know the quality of a partner until he performs. In business, actions speak louder than words. Your partners have to perform according to your specifications, but with a local twist because of specific knowledge in their country. If you enter a country with two or three partners and one does not live up to your expectations, you have the others with whom you can continue to build operations.

In order to enter with several partners, you could divide the country by cities or regions, or by specialties, by types of customers or by niches. There are numerous ways to do this, and it is best to tell potential partners up front that you are looking for two or three partners to open the country, and if they can refer others to you.

7) Manage each partner and each country correctly long term.

The entrepreneur always searches for change, responds to it and exploits it as an opportunity.
~ Peter Drucker

In each country, partners must be managed correctly with a long-term view. You must care for the goose that lays the golden eggs and tend to it correctly, depending on what it needs. You must understand the inner workings, strengths, weaknesses and personality of your partners, and be able to manage them correctly so that they can produce the results that you need. Partner companies and organizations are like people; they have personalities that must be understood and must be managed correctly in order to get results. In the end, you are only as successful as the people you have on your team, so manage partners correctly and with care.

CONCLUSION

Growing Globally Requires Action and Focus, and the Potential is Staggering

The only limits are those of vision.
~ James Broughton

With partner strategies, the potential to grow globally is staggering. It is profitable and rewarding, but it requires action and focus. You can leverage others' specific market knowledge, market contacts, and solutions. Incredible profit opportunities, expansion and influence emerge when you go global – changing many lives for the better.

These seven steps have been used over and over again to expand organizations overseas. The partner strategy is usually more effective than trying to set up operations in the country and learning from scratch. You need to use local in-country partners that have years of experience you can plug into and that already have the customers you want. There are many more complexities, and the execution requires the ability to interpret what you have found and make correct decisions, but the strategies work wonders and will bring you the results you want.

About Albert

Dr. Albert Allen, MBA, DBA, PhD, Lord of Crofton of London, is an industry expert in helping companies and organizations go into other countries, having done so for over 25 years for several dozens of companies in technology, investments, retail, food service, modernization, customs, property investment, non-profit, manufacturing, call centers, services, legal and education. The descendent of a Diplomatic and real estate/shipping family, he has lived and worked since childhood in Asia, Latin America, Europe and the Middle East taking companies global, developing influential government and business contacts, keen insight into cultures and specialized knowledge on how business is done overseas. Having worked with global multinationals expanding their operations overseas, he has unparalleled wealth of knowledge in growing operations and businesses in foreign countries – which has made him a savvy businessman, multimillionaire entrepreneur and commercial property investor.

As the current Lord of Crofton, a European title dating back to 1,192 with King Richard the Lion Heart and the Third Crusades, passed down through England's most successful magnates and businessmen with a heart to help others as quiet and unassuming philanthropists, Dr. Allen has held key and influential positions in business, philanthropy, government advising and trade development – including China Customs, China Chamber for Promotion of International Trade, PWC, Mexico Customs, Lockheed Martin, Public Warehousing Group, Inspection and Control Services, U.S. Chamber of Commerce, International Council of Shopping Centers, Prices Around the World, ICM and trade organizations in 26 different countries on three continents. He has taught at Tsinghua University/Harvard Program and Peking/Beda University and helped modernize customs and trade councils in 23 countries under the World Trade Organization.

Dr. Allen is an entrepreneur with a mission and has been involved in over 26 businesses and startups. He is considered a China expert, and resides between Washington, New York City and London. He is a best-selling author, international public speaker, has been invited to speak at the U.N. Headquarters in New York City, member of the National Academy of Best Selling Authors, Council Member of The Global Entrepreneurship Initiative, recipient of a Quilly award, participant at the Annual IMF and World Bank

Group Civil Society Policy Forum and member of the Thought Leader Summit.

In his free time, he enjoys reading, classical piano/cello, long-distance running/swimming, fishing, hunting and table tennis, but most of all being with his wife Alexandra and their two children, Alexandra and Andrew – with whom he is involved in funding and building over the last 14 years 1,150 children feeding centers, orphanages, children hope centers, churches, schools and clinics, in 27 countries with U.S. and in-country partners.

Albert is an active member of his church in the U.S. and overseas, and serves as a deacon, teaches children Sunday school and connects people to ministries. He sits on the board of several investment companies and nonprofits, where he lends his expertise in international operations, investments, and real estate.

You can connect with Dr. Allen at:
- albertallen@bartonyork.com
- (757) 912-3252 or (703) 431-6107
Washington DC, New York City, London

CHAPTER 13

MASTERING THE ART OF SELF

BY DAWN NIC, CHHC, CLC & CLORINDA CANELLI-PALANDRI, CLC

Balance, peace and joy are the fruit of a successful life.
It starts with recognizing your talents and finding ways to serve
others by using them.
~ Thomas Kinkade

What makes us so different than other life coaches out there? This is a question we often get and one we can easily answer. We are us. We are unique individuals; we have our own philosophy and our own approach to the way we choose to live our lives. We strive for balance, we choose compassion and empathy, we practice kindness and gratitude, and we are accountable to ourselves for our own happiness. Let me repeat that, *we are accountable to ourselves for our own happiness*. We have found that success starts with self; self-love, self-acceptance, self-awareness. Mastering the *Art of Self* breeds success in all areas of our lives.

What are you looking for?

When our clients come to us, it's because they are unfulfilled in certain areas of their lives. In saying that, we need to pose these questions to you. Are you happy? Do you find joy in your life? Are you satisfied with who you are? There is a difference is between happiness and joy. Happiness is extrinsic, meaning we look for outside sources to fill the void which elicits the feeling of happiness temporarily. Joy is intrinsic; it's a state of being— regardless of circumstance. Joy brings about inner peace. Which would you rather be, happy or joyful?

What is the Whole Self Approach™?

The Whole Self Approach™ is an approach to living your life in a manner that is going to bring about the best version of yourself. It's an approach centered around self. Once you have the ability to fully embrace yourself, you are now able to apply these skills in other areas of your life which helps to create balance. When you have balance, you think clearly, you are emotionally and physically healthier, and you are less stressed. Balance helps you to create the life you want to live, but most importantly to sustain it. Ultimately, our approach will gift you the insight and awareness to self and others, so that you may be able to live a more joyous and abundant life.

How do you define Success?

Success is personal to each individual. It is important that you know what your own definition of success is. For us, success means being able to live our truth, to be our authentic selves, and to empower others to do the same. We believe that every person has the ability to create the life they want to live. By utilizing our approach, we are giving you the tools to nourish the self in order to achieve a balance of mind, body and spirit. We believe in the Whole Self Approach™ of finding and maintaining balance in order to achieve a true state of success.

Success means achieving a balance in areas of our lives that affect daily living, such as relationships, health, finance, career, passion and spirituality. When we are balanced in these areas, it creates a center of peace within you. When you are at peace with yourself, your overall state of being changes to one of gratitude, compassion, empathy and forgiveness. This opens up the doors to change so you can create the life you want to live. Our goal here is to help you transition from the mindset of limited to limitless.

Success Starts with Self

Before we go on and introduce the Whole Self Approach™ that will help you to achieve your own success, we must tell you the following. It won't be easy. It can be painful at times. It will bring up fear and doubt. In order for you to master your own success, you must be willing to be honest with yourself. You must be committed to the process and you must be willing to do the work. We can say from our experience, mastering the art of self has brought us awareness on a level that helped us to live the lives we want to live. It has opened up opportunities in ways that has positively changed our lives. It brought us here on this journey with you and we are truly humbled and honored.

Self-Awareness

Take a look at the different areas mentioned above. Make sure you look at each area and identify the strengths and weakness in each one. Take a moment to ask yourself the following questions. Write down your answers so that you may revisit them continuously to do the work.

- What are the areas in your life that you feel are impeding your success?
- Within those areas, what are the obstacles preventing you from attaining your goals?
- What feelings are brought upon you as you identify the weaknesses?
- Can you pinpoint a time in your life where you had first experienced this feeling?

- Are there commonalities within specific areas of your life?
- Make a list of things that bring you joy.
- How much time do you spend doing the things you love?
- If you are no longer doing the things you love, what would you need to do in order to incorporate them into your life?

We know these are not easy questions. Do the best that you can. We are all works in progress and we are all on our own individual journey. Whenever you arrive, you are just in time.

Self-Acceptance

This is the most important step in our approach. Acceptance is the stepping stone to self-love. Only you can fill the void you may be feeling. You need to be able to accept where you are, at this point, without judgement. Acceptance means you are not living in the past. You can't change what has already happened. It's a done deal and it's time to leave it alone. Some are constantly in a state of worry about the future. The future does not exist. You cannot control the outcome of something that hasn't even happened yet. Do not create an environment of worry and anxiety for yourself. When you are living your life in the past or the future you are missing out on the present moment. In actuality, you are missing out on life and allowing opportunities to pass you by.

Once you accept yourself for exactly who you are and where you are, you can then make necessary changes. Many of the ideas we have about who we are, were formed during our childhood and reinforced as we grew up. Acceptance is not just about accepting your circumstances, it about accepting yourself. We call it mastering the art of self because we are our own worst critic.

Accepting yourself means not placing blame on yourself for your life's circumstance, rather to change your perspective on how you see your role in your life. Everything we do, has a purpose. We are exactly where we are supposed be right now. Everything you have done has brought you to this point. Accept it. Grow from it.

Take steps to change it. With acceptance, you are on the path to freedom from what has confined you.

An exercise we teach in our workshops on acceptance is what we call the mirror exercise:

- Stand in front of a mirror, take a good look at yourself and write down three things that you see.
- How did you describe yourself?
- Were the adjectives you used superficial?
- Now, make a list of how your best friend would describe you?
- Do you see how you may look at yourself compared to how others may view you?

It's all one and the same. Look for only positive things about yourself. If your list about yourself describes you physically, change your thought process and now describe who you are as a person. The goal is when you look at yourself in the mirror, it's to see the inner being, not the shell it comes in. Another exercise in acceptance is to utilize positive affirmations from which our thoughts become our beliefs, and our beliefs become our reality. Therefore, by incorporating positive affirmations and repeating them, we begin to shift our thoughts and beliefs about ourselves. You can post your affirmations somewhere you see them often. Each time you see them, it enters our subconscious mind. Write down a list of affirmations that will help you to have acceptance. Practice affirmations every day.

For example:
- I am worthy.
- I am exactly where I am supposed be right now.
- I commit to change.
- My circumstance doesn't define me.

Self-Love

Resentment is hard to live with. It is one of the reasons why we are stuck in negativity. Resentments are why we continuously live in the past. We focus on what went wrong in our lives or who has wronged us, that it's hard to move forward. Ask yourself, why are you holding on to resentments? What purpose does it serve you? Who is it hurting? We all know that holding on to resentments hurts us. So, why do we hold on? Does it go back to self-worth? Do you deserve to be free of resentment and anger? Anger comes in many forms, one being internalized anger. This is self-destructive as you do not have an outlet for your anger. Holding onto it only impedes your ability practice self-love. You have the power to let go. It's a choice.

How do you do that?

- Make a list of all the people you hold resentment or anger towards. Make sure you include yourself on this list. (It's only natural to resent yourself for allowing others to affect you negatively.)
- For each person, write out what the resentment is.
- How did this affect you?
- What role did they play in the situation?
- What role did you play?

Remember, there are two roles in every situation. Doing nothing is also a role that you play. You may hold resentment against yourself for doing nothing. Once you have done that, make a conscious decision to forgive them and yourself.

Forgiveness is the only cure to letting go of anger and resentment.

Forgiveness is something we often talk about with all clients. Most people do not realize that forgiveness is a completely selfish act, one that you should embrace. Forgiveness is all about self-love; therefore, the first person who needs forgiving is yourself.

Forgiveness doesn't mean you condone other people's behaviors, it means you are giving yourself permission to let go of the hurt that you feel from being wronged. Forgiveness is a choice.

You do not have to directly go to the person and say that you forgive them. If you want to, that's great, but it's not necessary to do so in order to allow yourself to be free from holding onto the resentment. Remember, this is for you. Forgiveness is not easy. You have to allow yourself to feel the pain. Know that you are not alone. Often people pray to ask for guidance in this process.

Here's an exercise to help you forgive:
• Find a quiet place.
• Write a letter to whomever you are choosing to forgive.

In this letter, it is important to state the following:
– I choose to forgive you.
– I no longer hold onto the anger or hurt.
– I am free of pain.
– I allow myself to move on.

Once this is complete, you may share this letter with someone you trust or you can choose to burn the letter. The actual act of burning the letter is freeing and cathartic.

When we are free of the emotions that prevent us from loving ourselves, we have the ability to allow gratitude to come into our hearts. When this happens we feel compassion and empathy for ourselves as well as others. This changes our perspective in the way we see ourselves, and how we view our role in different areas of our lives. When you are able to identify your role, you are able to elicit change and help yourself find balance.

RECAP

What does the approach do for me? The Whole Self Approach™ gives you the insight to see the role you play in each of the areas of self-awareness, self-acceptance and self-love. When you master the *Art of Self*, you are able to bring about positive change into all areas of your life. Fear naturally subsides as you understand yourself better, and as you embrace change, it empowers you to have self-belief. We believe it's a practice. It does not come naturally to always think of 'self' first, but it's something you can nurture and continually work on. Our goal for you, as with all our clients, is for you to lead a life that is fulfilling. We want you to live, not exist. Your possibilities are limitless. So, always remember:

- Be kind
- Be compassionate
- Have empathy
- Practice gratitude
- Communicate your desires clearly
- Embrace change
- Believe in yourself
- Take action towards your goal
- Always be self-aware and accountable
- Live your truth

Be kind to yourself and others always!
Live your life with Joy, Love and Care!
~ Dawn and Clorinda

About Dawn & Clorinda

Dawn Nic, CHHC, CLC is a co-founder of Whole Self Approach, LLC. She is a certified Life Coach and Health Coach. Dawn has co-developed the Whole Self Approach™ training program and co-authored self-help workbooks. She co-created the Happiness Workshop which has helped thousands of people find their meaning of true joy. She is a motivational speaker as well as an expert in addiction counseling. Dawn is the co-host of Live Your Truth with Whole Self Approach™ radio show. She is in the process of co-writing her second book, *Whole Self Approach™ to Healthy Living* with Clorinda.

Clorinda Canelli-Palandri, CLC is a co-founder of Whole Self Approach, LLC. She is a certified Life Coach and Reiki Master. Clorinda has co-developed the Whole Self Approach™ training program and co-authored self-help workbooks. She co-created the Happiness Workshop which has helped thousands of people find their meaning of true joy. Clorinda has written and recorded meditations. She is the co-host of Live Your Truth with Whole Self Approach™ radio show. She is in the process of co-writing her second book, *Whole Self Approach™ to Healthy Living* with Dawn. She lives in New York with her two daughters.

CHAPTER 14

THE GIFT OF LIGHTNING STRIKES AS ONE PREPARES TO BE A MENTOR AND COACH

BY BILL TRUESDALE, Ed.D.

It is your decisions, not your conditions,
that determine your future.
~ Tony Robbins.

The gift of lightning strikes shapes us to be better decision makers as coaches and mentors. In education, as in life, there is a need to be mentored and coached as we juggle the many variables that come our way. These variables can't always be controlled – they strike like lightning. So how do we manage our decisions in the face of these large strikes?

Taking a tour into the desert near the San Andreas Fault in Southern California is one of those experiences of a lifetime. The desert is beautiful, silent, and a spiritual place to reflect. The palm trees that live there are strong, majestic, and tower over this dry bed of land like a protective canopy. You probably have heard about the San Andreas Fault, which extends for about

600 miles or 965 km, that some say will threaten California's attachment to the United States. When life's routine changes, the thought of the San Andreas Fault becomes my metaphor for my new normal.

The San Andreas Fault forms the tectonic boundary between the Pacific Plate and the North American Plate and its motion is a right lateral strike slip that moves horizontally. The transform fault has two plates moving in opposite directions. The opposite directions can represent our belief systems: the limiting beliefs about the meaning of adversity moving away from and the empowering beliefs of adversity moving towards a greater good and purpose. However, the Fault is divided into three sections, each with different characteristics and a different degree of earthquake risk; we all live on faults, maybe not 600 miles long, but faults all the same.

We walk along in a job we've had for years and years. I served in public education as a teacher, assistant principal and principal in the same urban school district for 26 years, an urban elementary school principal at the same school for 12 years, and then lightning strikes and boom . . . we get downsized, outsized, and criticized. No earthquake, not yet. It's one of the sections of the fault line; but not enough to cause damage. The reason for one's ability to experience this tremor and manage the aftershocks resides in one's self-efficacy. Self-efficacy is one's notion in trusting themselves enough to reinvent and learn from past experiences.

The desert palm trees are a perfect example and symbol of how resiliency drives life's adjustments. The palm trees are angiosperms and produce a wide variety of fruits and berries. There are two types of fruit-bearing palm trees that can be observed in this desert. One type of palm tree has never been struck by lightning (yes, it does rain in the desert, and lightning does strike – sometimes without rain). The other type of palm tree has been struck by lightening repeatedly. The palm tree that has been hit by lightning many times is My Hero. That palm tree that is repeatedly struck by lightning produces more fruit and is at times healthier. Nature provided me with a valuable gift and a metaphor for mastering my own challenges.

I believe and trust myself. There were the aftershocks and lightning storms in my life – parental loss (my father died of a heart attack when I was seven years old), struggling financially to put myself through undergraduate and graduate school, a near-fatal car accident, a shoulder and knee injury due to weight lifting that still hurts when the weather changes, true love-relationship losses, and the loss of a job – which were all challenging. I believe that God has a higher purpose for those aftershocks and lightning storms in my life. That gift is to share my skills and experience as I mentor and coach others. Additionally, I am currently completing national mentor certification for principals. The truths that guide my notions of mentoring and coaching include: understand and be understood, adjust and readjust, listen and speak with respect, be the palm tree struck by lightning in the desert bearing more fruit, living in spite of faults, building relationships for community and collaboration, finding humor in my life with sunshine, leaving a legacy and passing on the torch.

For this brief discussion, let us define the terms. A mentor is a person who is available to listen and suggest strategies for decision-making. It is assumed that a mentor has EXPERIENCE and EXPERTISE in the particular field. The mentor must be carefully vetted before they offer support to the person who seeks suggestions and guidance. A coach, on the other hand, functions as a person who helps another improve their skills and performance outcomes. It is assumed that a coach KNOWS the detailed construction of the major task. That coach, it is assumed, can isolate certain challenges and offer substantive feedback that defines possible decisions and produces quality outcomes for the client.

There is a dance that unfolds. A person who seeks a mentor, usually chooses a mentor partner that hears the rhythm of the challenge(s) and one who can prevent the client from stepping on too many toes. The coach makes sure the client can execute the dance steps. At any rate, there is a reciprocity between anyone who seeks coaching or mentoring and the coach/mentor.

Eight Steps to be an effective Mentor and Coach include:

1. Understand and be understood
2. Adjust and readjust
3. Listen and speak with respect
4. Be the palm tree struck by lightning in the desert
5. Living in spite of faults
6. Building relationships for community and collaboration
7. Finding the humor in one's life with sunshine
8. Leaving a legacy and passing on the torch

Step 1. Understand and be Understood

The basis of all communication is its reciprocal nature. There are many ways that communication is manifested: body language, being on time, returning phone calls, responding to emails, tweets, and so on. Coaches must understand the nature of the challenge(s) by 'watching' the communication habits. Mentors must understand the nature of the challenge(s) by understanding the antecedents and consequences of what needs to be decided. Mentors and coaches must also tell the client (person who is seeking support) how they want to be treated.

Step 2. Adjust and Readjust

Brainstorming strategies are the center of meaningful dialogue and discussion in problem solving. The mentor/coach can develop structures that lead to intentionality of the decisions to be made. For example: Would you like more information on ... Do you think you could use some resources such as ... A couple of things to keep in mind are ... Sometimes it may be helpful to ... . What you are saying and how it is said. Howard Gardner, a noted psychologist (1983), says: "There are seven styles of learning: (1) visual/spatial – prefers using pictures, images, and spatial understanding;

(2) aural/auditory – prefers to hear information; (3) musical – prefers using sound and rhythm; (4) verbal/linguistic – prefers using words, both in speech and writing; (5) bodily /kinesthetic – prefers using their body, hands, and sense of touch; (6) solitary intrapersonal – prefers to use self-study and social interpersonal – prefers to learn in groups with other people; and (7) logical/ mathematical – prefers using logic, reasoning, and systems." It is important for any coach or mentor to adjust and readjust to the client's learning style. The coach/mentor must take the time to get to know the client.

Step 3. Listen and Speak with Respect
The heart of mentoring and coaching is listening and speaking with respect. The ability to speak with openness and honesty with each other is the key in earning trust. To resolve conflicts and disagreements respectfully without becoming disagreeable requires a tacit respect to acknowledge different perspectives. The mentor/coach must assure the client of confidentiality.

Step 4. Be the Palm Tree Struck by Lightning in the Desert
The mentor/coach symbolizes the palm tree struck by lightning in the desert. The mentor/coach must show the client that lightning offers challenges that can be overcome. The mentor/coach has lived these experiences and can give off the fruit of knowledge in creativity, connectivity, and competence. The resiliency of the palm tree that has been struck by lightning is a metaphor for not giving up and learning from those aftershocks and lightning strikes. The client must 'see' rebirth, regrowth and rejuvenation.

Step 5. Living in Spite of Faults
The mentor/coach needs to understand that he/she has both strengths and weaknesses as does his/her client. Michael Jackson sang a song about the man looking in the mirror, he must tell himself the truth. The mentor/coach must be honest enough to have the client use his/her strengths to remediate the limitations that affect the consequences of the decisions to be made. The client will also tell the mentor/coach what is not working for them.

Step 6. Building Relationships for Community and Collaboration

No man is an island; every man is a piece of the continent,
a part of the main...
~ John Donne.

No man/woman stands alone. Every person is intertwined into the cloth of humanity. We are all part of a larger community of learners and teachers. We must combine our assets to manage our challenges. For example, in education, a professional learning community is a systematic process wherein teachers, parents and administrators work together to analyze and improve their practice with students and other stakeholders. We must work in teams, engaging in an ongoing cycle of questions that promote deeper team learning that will define clear goals. The mentor/ coach and client are engaged in identifying clear targets/goals, making thoughtful decisions, developing benchmarks to create timelines, responsibilities, and accomplishments, and gathering human resources to help manage the challenges and celebrate the success.

Step 7. Finding Humor in One's Life with Sunshine

The mentor/coach must remind the client of what's really important in their life: their interpretation of the meaning of the experience. For example, you will perhaps have heard this old story illustrating the difference between positive thinking and negative thinking. Many years ago, there were two salesmen sent by a British shoe manufacturer to Africa to investigate and report back on market potential. The first salesman reported back, "There is no potential here, nobody wears shoes." The second salesman reported back, "There is massive potential here, nobody wears shoes."

Step 8. Leaving a Legacy and Passing on the Torch

The mentor/coach LEARNS from every experience. The client learns from every experience. The optimal result from these interactions is that everyone builds a repertoire of evidence-based strategies that work. After the mentoring and coaching is all said and done, and the client makes decisions to accomplish the target goals, then comes the self-assessment. Client, Mentor, Coach engage in reflection with some suggested ways to see the value of the decisions in the experience:

- What was the most effective strategy?
- What was the least effective strategy?
- What are your strengths?
- What are your deficiencies?
- What follow-up work is needed?
- To what extent has your performance improved over time?
- How does your preferred learning style influence your decisions?
- What do you really understand about_____?
- What questions/uncertainties do you still have about _____?
- What are the observable indicators of success?

The decisions we make affect our conditions. You can choose to be alone or you can call on your community (mentors/ coaches). Know that your community, your conversations and your collaborative activities enable you to weigh your decisions before you make them. In the desert of our lives, most of us endure some lightning strikes. Nature offers a metaphor through the palm trees that have been hit the most – they bear the most fruit and are the healthiest. Aftershocks are manageable, and I can present myself as a mentor and/or a coach because I am one of the palm trees hit by lightning – my aftershock is a new career.

About Bill

Bill Truesdale helps his clients become more effective leaders by navigating the changing dynamics of an organization. Bill's passion is to help develop the knowledge, skills and technical skills of new principals to become effective school leaders. Effective school leaders positively impact the lives of our most precious resource in the United States, the education of our children.

Bill began his twenty-six-year journey in the world of education serving as a substitute teacher, a teacher, an assistant principal and a principal in the Chicago Public Schools. He also teaches as an adjunct professor of Educational Administration at Chicago State University. Bill serves on the Governing Board of the Principal Preparation program at Chicago State University.

Bill's focus on serving as a mentor is his philosophy using a quote from Michael Angelo, "I saw an Angel in the stone and I set it free." His goal is to bring out the natural strengths of his clients and develop their leadership style as influencers, doers, relators and thinkers. Bill also focuses on having his clients use the seven learning styles to communicate and lead organizations to success.

Bill has earned a Doctorate in Education from Loyola University in Chicago and two Master's degrees. The first was in Exercise Physiology from the University of Illinois at Chicago and the second was in Education (Special Education) from Chicago State University. He has also earned an undergraduate degree in teaching from the University of Illinois at Chicago. Bill has earned six Illinois teaching certificates and completed a two-year portfolio pilot study on Principals.

Bill was recognized by the National Board of Professional Teaching Standards. His school, Douglas Taylor, has been recognized nationally by the N.A.S.S.P. as a Met-Life Break Through School in 2008, and Re-Designated Break Through School in 2013, and featured in an Edition of *Principal Leadership Magazine*. Bill is the author of the book, *The Implementation of Peer Coaching on the Transferability of Staff Development to Classroom Practice*. This was the first study of peer coaching in the Chicago Public Schools. Bill is a coauthor of the new book, *Breaking Ranks: Focus on Leaders*, collaborating with the N.A.S.S.P. (National Association Secondary School and Middle School Principals Association). The book will be published in 2017 and be distributed at the National Principal Convention.

Bill Truesdale is a speaker and has presented on the Breaking Ranks Model at both the state and national level. He is also a member of The City Club of Chicago—Illinois' premier public affairs forum since 1903. He is completing national certification as a principal mentor with the N.A.E.S.P. (National Association of Elementary School Principals). He has completed the National Superintendents Academy. He is also a former national competitive powerlifter and has coached Special Olympic Powerlifting. Bill is an advocate for health, fitness, and a natural master bodybuilder.

You can connect with Bill at:
- LinkedIn: Bill Truesdale
- Twitter: @wttruesdale
- www.facebook.com/Bill Truesdale
- Email: billtruesdale2@gmail.com
- Website: DrBillTruesdalemanagementandconsulting.net

CHAPTER 15

CHOOSING TO LIVE HERE IN VITALITY

BY JASON STEPHENSON

I started my twenties as a budding vocalist, and finished them with anxiety, depression and a drug addiction.

In my 20's and 30's I was a singer, performing in various clubs and talent quests across Australia, Taiwan and Malaysia. I was good at what I did, and I loved it. I often took first place in the Grand Finals, or at the very least second or third. Every night, I was in the zone, savouring the spotlight and revelling in the audience's applause.

But talent contests do not pay ongoing bills. Although I was 'going great guns' in the talent contest field, it transitioned into very little professional work. Work was scarce, and when it did appear, all too often it would fall through at the last moment. I took it lightly at first, but it began to wear me down.

Month after month, still no work came in. I was despondent, angry and hurt that my dreams were thwarted, no matter how much work I put in. I switched to the victim mode. "Why me?" I would often say. "I'm a good guy. Why can't I achieve my dreams? I'm not asking too much, am I?" After a while, I began to feel that my skills weren't good enough for the professional level, and I was stuck forever as a talent contestant. It wasn't true, but I believed it. And I didn't just believe it—I let it dictate my feelings and actions.

Things became more dire. Before too long, I could no longer cover my bills, and had to sign up for unemployment benefits or face being thrown out of my rental property. Before, I had felt trapped and oppressed—but now, I felt worthless.

Again, my negative experiences dictated my actions. I turned to alcohol and drugs to ease the pain, going on weekend benders that often ended in bed with a stranger. For a while, it was a fun way to hide from my inner turmoil. For a while, even numbness was better than pain. And the deeper this destructive spiral took me, the deeper I wanted to go.

Before too long, the effects started to show, but I refused to acknowledge them. I started resenting what others had. I betrayed some friends and treated others unfairly. I gleefully abused my body, mind and spirit in every way I could. It didn't seem like a problem. I had fallen so far that I no longer cared—for myself or anyone around me.

After several drug- and alcohol-fuelled years, the abuse began to take its toll on me. I felt sick, tired, and run down on every level. Seeing my friends held no appeal. All I wanted was to stay indoors and in bed for days at a time, laying in the darkness and hiding from the truth. For although my body and mind were ravaged, my spirit knew something was amiss. After much deliberation, I mustered the energy to go for a medical check-up. One simple visit changed my life forever.

Two weeks after my appointment, I received a call from my doctor. His voice was calm, the results conclusive. I was HIV positive.

Everything stopped. I fell into a deep, dark space, and I stayed there. Every mention of HIV reminded me that I was immune deficient. I was a walking time bomb, waiting to detonate at any moment. "Don't worry, people with HIV are living for 7-10 years now," my counsellor told me—but the information did nothing. I was inconsolable.

Although I was supposed to be focused on healing, my body and spirit deteriorated even further. Simple activities became nearly impossible. For months, I couldn't face anyone. I felt ashamed, guilty, worthless, and scared. In short, I felt deficient.

Twelve months passed. I struggled. I persevered. And then, one sunny day, as I walked across a sandy beach near my home, it hit me. I was alive! My two dogs, Buddy and Dharma, splashed in the waves, and above me, brilliant white clouds sailed across a turquoise sky. A warm breeze caressed my skin, and for the first time in a year, I felt truly alive.

In that moment, I was not deficient in any way, shape or form. I had woken from a long sleep. In fact, in that moment, I was not just alive, I was living. Right there, right then, I was living in vitality.

From that day forward, I decided the term HIV would stand for "Here In Vitality" rather than "human immunodeficiency virus." I vowed to make the abbreviation empowering instead of limiting—a reminder that despite everything, I was alive, well and living in vitality. I chose to reject the term 'deficiency' and its connotations of scarcity, limitations, and weakness. HIV became a positive affirmation, a clinical diagnosis transformed into a beautiful reminder of my own power and life – *here in vitality.*

Each day, I chanted, "I am living *here in vitality*" as I walked my dogs along the beach. I wrote the affirmation down, stuck it on bathroom mirror, and read it daily. Each time I repeated the phrase, I felt it in every fibre of my being. New energy blossomed within me. A simple phrase reminded me to focus on the beauty of the present moment. I felt alive.

As I regained my energy, I realized it was time to give back to society instead of taking from it. Inspired by my own experience with affirmations, I produced a children's CD called, "I Believe In Me." – harnessing affirmation words, songs, and a guided meditation to help kids believe in themselves at a young age—and to recognise that they are valuable no matter what they choose to do in life. As I recorded the CD, I found that I had a knack for the spoken word, and I decided to start sharing more affirmations and guided meditations with the world.

Today, my YouTube channel has over 470,000 subscribers and I work for myself full-time as a meditation artist. I get the opportunity to speak at engagements around the world, inspiring people to live more in the moment and with optimism. I have recorded over 150 guided meditations to help others who suffer with depression, anxiety, PTSD and stress live with more joy in their lives. I feel happier, calmer, and more at peace—and in a way, I am fulfilling my dream of being a performance artist. My wishes have come true in a way I never could have predicted. I always thought I was "Jason the singer" – and so when I could not get work as a singer, I felt like my identity was 'unemployed' and allowed myself to fall apart. I felt worthless.

Now of course, I realize we are human beings, not human *doings*. We are greater than our actions, greater than ourselves. I am elated to wake up each day, but it was not always this way. It took a tragedy to bring me to this place of joy—but the same does not have to be true of you.

I have shared my story, but I would like to share some of the lessons we have glossed over during that long, challenging process of finding vitality instead of disease. My spiritual and physical recovery was not instantaneous. Each day, I worked to find healing and peace. Each hour, day, week, and year had its ups and downs, but today I am happy to be living with even better health and vitality than ever before!

If you, too, are struggling to find a vibrant and contented life, perhaps my four cornerstones to vitality can help. Applied with a little compassion each day, they will lighten your burden and illuminate your way toward happiness.

Cornerstone # 1: Take 100% ownership of what happens in your life – both internally and externally. Remember that you have the power to control your reaction to any event, shaping even a poor outcome into a beautiful lesson.

Cornerstone # 2: Start meditating daily. Set aside five or ten minutes to sit in silence or listen to a guided meditation. Understand that thoughts will come and go as you go, as you breathe, but remember that this is all a part of the process. Eventually, you will become aware of the thoughts, whereupon you can simply acknowledge their presence and return your attention to your breathing. You don't have to 'try' to meditate. In fact, meditation is best done without trying. Simply be. This is enough.

When we sit quietly and connect to only our breathing and find stillness within the moment, we realize that we are more than just our bodies. We can transcend all space and time. In fact, time no longer exists when we meditate. We only have now. This exact moment. And in this moment, we are everything. We have all we need, right here, right now. We are connected to everything and everyone that is or ever was. We are at peace.

Cornerstone # 3: Do your best to live in gratitude. Be truly grateful for today. Since my fateful diagnosis and breakthrough, I have realized that the more gratitude I express, the more I am showered with love, joy, and finances. With gratitude, I no longer look for what I can get out of life—I look for what I can give!

As you begin your own journey towards gratitude, start by expressing your delight at being here today. For waking up and having a chance to help change others' lives. For being you, even if it is difficult. Remember, today is the first day of the rest of your life. Open your heart to even more abundance, and trust that when you do, the universal flood gates will open and give you more.

Cornerstone # 4: **Use affirmations.** Even a set of simple statements can transform your life. Speak them out loud. Write them down. Really feel them. By using affirmations, you begin to replace negative thoughts with positivity and hope. Start with statements like, "I am living in abundance." or "I live every day with gratitude." or "My life is beautiful, and I am too." to get started. Or, choose an affirmation that resonates with you.

As frightening as the future may be, we must remember that today is all we have. We can't change yesterday or dictate what tomorrow will bring. We cannot always prevent disease or ensure success. What we can do is realize that in this moment, we have the power to change our responses to the events that occur within our lives. We have the power to shift our lives from victim mode to a winner's way, expressing love and gratitude for everything that exists in this very moment. You are strong. You are powerful. And like me, you have the power to live each moment—*Here in Vitality.*

About Jason

Jason Stephenson is the founder of Relax Me Online Australia Pty Ltd (an online MP3-guided meditation site), and has been involved in the meditation/relaxation music field for the past 15 years. His YouTube Meditation Sleep Music Channel has grown to over 470,000 subscribers and has had over one hundred million views.

Jason has spoken and performed on an international level in Australia, U.S.A., Taiwan and Malaysia. He performed winning songs in an International Buddhist song contest, "Sounds of the Human World" in 2005 and 2006.

Recently, Jason completed his Usui Reiki First Degree Certificate and has completed a Diploma of Neuro-Psychological Immunity (H & H College, Queensland, Australia) — a course where Jason says, "I really began to understand the power and connection between health of the mind and body." Currently Jason is studying the "Success Principles" with Jack Canfield's Online Train the Trainer course.

Jason resides in a small sea-side town on the east cost of NSW Australia with his two faithful   companion dogs, Buddy and Dharma.

Russell Brand (UK Comedian/Activist) has recently spoken highly of Jason's guided meditations stating: "Try some of Jason's amazing meditation techniques. Allow this gentle Australian brain alchemist to dabble in your semi-conscious brain."

You can connect with Jason at:
- www.jasonstephenson.net
- www.facebook.com/jasonstephensonmeditation

CHAPTER 16

STRATEGIC INVESTING

BY HARRY SMITH

As a financial advisor for more than three-decades, I am often asked, "Where is the best place to invest my money right now?" People are usually surprised by my response, "How you behave as an investor is more important than what you invest in."

Evidence for counterproductive investor behavior can be found in the annual DALBAR studies.[1] Since 1994, DALBAR's Quantitative Analysis of Investor Behavior (QAIB) has been measuring the effects of investor decisions to buy, sell and switch into and out of mutual funds over both short and long-term time frames. The results consistently show that the average investor earns less – in many cases, much less – than mutual fund performance reports would suggest. As Benjamin Graham, the father of value investing said; "The investor's chief problem – and even his worst enemy – is likely to be himself." An important step to becoming a more successful investor is to develop a better understanding why our brains may be working against us.

You may have seen the Shepard's table illusion before. The illusion was first identified by cognitive scientist Roger Shepard. The question is; "Which table is longer, the narrow one on the left or the fat one on the right?" Your brain is telling you that the table on the left is longer, and even if we measure both to prove that they are the same length - the one on the left still looks longer.

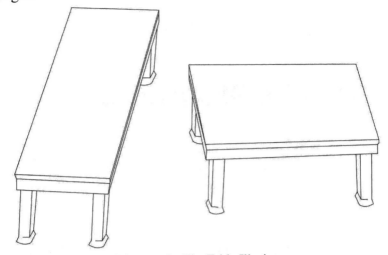

Diagram 1 - The Table Illusion

Dan Ariely, professor of Behavioral Economics at Duke and a behavioral economist, put it like this in a recent TED talk[2]: "Our intuition is fooling us in repeatable, predictable, and consistent ways – and there is almost nothing we can do about it. So, if we make these mistakes with vision, which in theory we are pretty good at and a significant portion of our brain is dedicated to, what's the chance that we don't make even more mistakes in areas we're not as good at – for example, financial decision making? Whether or not we think we make good financial decisions, or poor ones, we assume we're in control of the decisions we do make - but science would suggest that we are not."

There are two systems that operate in our brains. System one is instinctual and is good at handling large amounts of data rapidly and gives answers that are approximately correct. System one uses mental shortcuts to process information more rapidly. While system two, the higher reasoning part of our brain, requires deliberate effort, it handles one step at a time and it's a slow way for dealing with information. Psychological biases that influence all of us arise from how these two systems interact.

CYCLE OF MARKET EMOTIONS

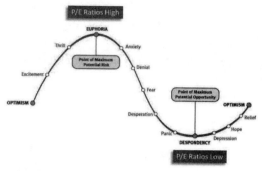

Source: RBC Wealth Management

Diagram 2 - Cycle of Market Emotions

We can see changing investor behavior in the financial markets, reflected in changing valuations. Historically, investors on average pay $16 for $1 of profits (this is commonly referred to as price/earnings, or P/E ratio). Interest rates, economic growth and other conditions can affect P/E ratios. But, when emotions run hot and the investing public becomes euphoric, valuations are higher. Conversely when emotions run cold and investors are despondent, valuations tend to shrink.

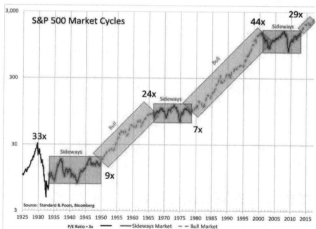

Diagram 3 - Market Cycles

The chart immediately above shows the past several market cycles going back to the 1930's. You might notice a pattern here, a 16-18-year sideways market, followed by a 16-18-year bull market.

Valuations at the beginning of the post-World War II bull market in 1949 were 9-times earnings and peaked at 24-times earnings in 1966 at the end of the bull market. The great bull market of the 80's and 90's began with a valuation of roughly 7-times earnings before peaking in 2000 at the height of the tech-bubble at 44-times earnings.

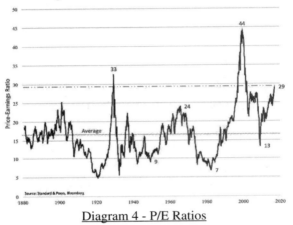

Diagram 4 - P/E Ratios

The chart above, shows P/E ratios for the U.S. market going back to the late 1800s. Bull markets are born during eras of lower valuations and mature at higher valuations. Legendary investor Sir John Templeton summed it up best when he said; "Bull markets are born on pessimism, grown on skepticism, mature on optimism and die on euphoria. The time of maximum pessimism is the best time to buy, and the time of maximum optimism is the best time to sell."

Here are just a few of the many cognitive biases that scientists have identified:

OVERCONFIDENCE / CONFIRMATION BIAS

How good of a driver are you? In surveys, 80% of drivers consider themselves to be above average. How good of a lover are you? If you are like most people you will answer above average, much like Garrison Keillor's Lake Woebegone – "where all the children are above average." Also, we tend to surround ourselves with information that validates our own point of view and dismiss input that conflicts with our reasoning.

I observed these biases recently in a couple in their late 50's with $2 million in personal savings earning very low returns in a savings account. In 2011, they pulled the money out of the stock market on a hunch that the market would decline, and remain in cash until this day. Had they left the money in the market, it would have grown to more than $3.9 million by 2017. That extra $1.9 millions of growth would have been enough to make up for their savings shortfall. An experienced risk manager would never make such a large one-way bet without hedging against other possible outcomes.

THE ENDOWMENT EFFECT / STATUS QUO BIAS / ATTACHMENT BIAS

My friend purchased wine from Bordeaux in the late 80's. He paid $20 per bottle for the 1989 Haut Brion on a futures contract. It turned out to be one of the wines of the century and today retails for $1,400 bottle. What should my friend do? Sell the wine and purchase more bottles of a less expensive wine? Keep what he has? Buy more of the same at $1,400/bottle? The endowment effect predicts that he will keep the bottles because he feels the wine is worth more than $1,400 and yet he will not pay that price to buy more.

In 2007, Washington Mutual Bank (WaMu) had a successful reputation dating back over one-hundred-years, and by 2008 became the largest bank failure in US history. In 2003, WaMu made a strategic decision to focus on subprime lending. In August 2007, with WaMu trading at $40, I met with a group of WaMu managers all with significant portions of their net worth invested in WaMu shares that they received in the form of stock grants. These managers were convinced it would go higher. By early February 2008, with the shares at $20, these holders were convinced this was temporary setback and the shares were worth more. By May of 2008, with the share price at $10, the story now focused on rumors that JP Morgan would buy WaMu, so the shares had to be worth more. By September, the company went into receivership and the shares today are worthless and JP Morgan assumed the leftovers.

THE DISPOSITION EFFECT / COGNITIVE DISSONANCE

People avoid actions that create regret and seek actions that cause pride. Regret is the emotional state that comes from previous bad decisions. Pride is the emotional state arising from good decisions.

Have you ever noticed that no one talks about their losers and everyone loves to talk about their winners? Research shows that even our memories are impacted, and as time progresses, our brains re-write history to avoid regret.

MENTAL ACCOUNTING

There is an apocryphal story known as the legend of the man in the green bathrobe – some in Las Vegas swear this is a true story. A newlywed man put on a robe in his suite and finds a $5 chip with the number 17 printed on it, which he takes as a sign. Being bored, he ventures out to the roulette table and bets the $5 chip on the number 17, and wins. The 35:1 bet pays $175. He bets the $175 on the number 17 and wins $6,125 and so it went until his winnings totaled $262 million. On the final roll, the number came up 18 and he lost everything. When he returned to his suite his wife asks; "Where have you been?" "Playing roulette," he answers. "How did you do?" she asks. "Not bad, I lost five-dollars."

Wait a minute, regardless if the story is true, he lost $262 million, not $5! Our mind tends to put windfall amounts into a separate mental bucket that treats those funds as being different than money we might earn. Whether we receive money in an inheritance, through a fortunate business venture or because one of our investments paid off in a big way, we need to think of that windfall in the same way that we do about money that we earn with the sweat of our brow.

REPRESENTATIVENESS

Our brains are quite good at pattern recognition. The brain makes assumptions that things that share similar qualities are quite alike, regardless of whether the assumption is true.

In 1998 and 1999, I ran across numerous situations where individuals had invested money in companies whose names ended with dot-com, without knowing what the company did. This was during the technology bubble, a time when any company with dot-com as part of its name meant the company had to be something special, much like the go-go era of the 60's when Telex, Xerox, Polaroid and Control Data were the dot-com equivalents of that era. One popular example was pets.com – largely due to its unique marketing campaign featuring sock puppets with appearances in Macy's Thanksgiving Parade and the Super Bowl. But the company was a spectacular failure and lost money on every sale. The company was founded in 1998, went public in February 2000 and liquidated 268 days after going public.

Here are eight tips to help protect you against these cognitive errors that we are all subject to:

1) Identify and understand behavioral biases. Remember these biases are affecting professional investors as well as amateurs. Identifying these biases can go a long way to making you a more successful investor.

2) Know why you are investing. Money is important, but what money can do for you is more important. Develop specific

measurable financial goals. Focus on the long-term and be realistic about whether your behavior supports your goals.

3) Investing is a marathon, not a sprint. Avoid that feeling of needing to get back to even. When you make investment decisions you are making the best decision that you can with the information that is available to you at that time. Cut your losers short and allow your winners to run.

4) Avoid seeking information that only confirms your point of view. Seek out trusted opinions that can work as a "devil's advocate" to consider a greater range of possible outcomes. Imagine that you only had cash to invest and if so, would you make a specific investment with that cash at this moment?

5) Establish quantitative investment criteria. Having a specific set of investment criteria will help you to avoid investing based on emotion, rumor, stories and other psychological biases. If you don't know what those investment criteria should be, then seek out guidance from a professional.

6) Real diversification helps you to avoid tragic losses. Real diversification is not owning a collection of mutual funds where 60% of the holdings are overlapping. True diversification means owning things that in times of crisis help to limit or even offset losses from more risky parts of your portfolio. If you don't understand what those types of investments are, then seek out professional help.

7) Control your investing environment. If you are a recovering alcoholic, hanging out in bars may not be a good idea or if you are on a diet, sitting at a table with a plate of warm, fragrant, chocolate chip cookies may not be helpful. I have seen investors who access their account value more than 20-times a day. Check your stocks once a month. Trade once a month. Monitor and review your portfolio performance quarterly.

8) Avoid being caught up in fads. The four most dangerous words on Wall Street are: "This time is different."

Reference Notes:
1. https://dalbar.com/QAIB/Index
2. https://embed.ted.com/talks/dan_ariely_asks_are_we_in_control_of_our_own_ decisions

About Harry

Harry Smith has more than 33-years of experience working with clients to create long-term, personalized, financial plans designed to help clients stay on track to accomplish their financial goals. Harry also is involved in overseeing investment selection and the portfolio design process. He is a Senior Vice President – Financial Advisor, and a Senior Portfolio Manager – Portfolio Focus, with RBC Wealth Management in Seattle, Washington.

Harry is a Chartered Retirement Planning Counselor® (CRPC®), having completed the certification through the College for Financial Planning in Denver, CO. He is a Certified Investment Management Analyst® (CIMA®), having completed his certification through the Investment Management Consultant Association's (IMCA) program at the Haas School of Business at the University of California, Berkeley. The CIMA® designation is awarded through the Investment Management Consultants Association®. He is a graduate of the Financial Advisors Leadership Program at the Wharton School at the University of Pennsylvania. His comments have been published in *Inc. Magazine, Forbes Magazine, Washington CEO Magazine, Seattle Magazine, Seattle Met Magazine* and *The Seattle Times.*

He has been recognized locally and nationally by the National Association of Board Certified Advisory Practices (NABCAP) and received recognition in the category of Client Education and Customer Service Model. He has been a guest instructor for the personal financial planning course with the MBA program at Seattle University. He has been a guest speaker and volunteer with the Evelyn Brust Financial Research and Education Foundation.

Harry Smith has worked with a number of community service programs including the U.S. Soccer Foundation, Washington State Youth Soccer Association, Washington State University's College of Agriculture, Human and Natural Resource Sciences (CAHNRS). He currently serves as a board member for the Bellevue Police Foundation.

Harry is a Seattle native. He and his wife of 39-years have three adult children.

CHAPTER 17

DEARLY BELOVED

BY DR. EDNA JOYCE C. SANTOS, MD, DPBO, SBO

Dearly Beloved,

We are writing to you from the Universe to let you know that you are incredibly loved.

We have been with you since your inception and we have surrounded you with the brilliance of our unconditional love. You are a magnificent human being whom we have enveloped with an aura of pure energy and genuine love which, when harnessed, would give you a powerful connection with the Divine.

We have never left you, but you have let your doubts and fears cloud the inner recesses of your mind and heart, letting them take over your whole being. You have unconsciously severed your connection with us with your increasing isolation and despair. You have let negative thoughts take over your most powerful tool ... your subconscious mind. You have completely forgotten how it is to live and be one with the Universe.

Do you remember what it was like to be a pristine child ... wandering with wide-eyed innocence as you played in gardens of delight, the silence broken only by angelic laughter. You were curious in every turn ... highly inquisitive at the vastness of the universe. You stared in awe at the beautiful butterflies and flocks of birds that flew high above ... gazed at the moon and stars as they illuminated the dark sky.

You are a child of the Universe, sincerely beloved and immensely treasured. Do not despair for we have always been here for you. You are not alone in your despondent search for inner peace that has somehow eluded you in your quest for the truth. We have heard your pleas and your zealous desire to belong, and be relieved of the burdens that have weighed you down all through these years.

We know that it has been sometime since you have seen the sun shining so brightly in your life. You feel the walls closing in around you everywhere you turn. You are drowning in a sea of misfortune that made you believe in your heart that bad luck followed you wherever you go.

Yet have you ever lifted your face up and seen the clouds clearing up in the sky? Have you ever seen the sun's rays peeping out from the dark clouds? Have you ever, for one moment, stilled the voices inside your head, and listened intently to the whispers of your heart?

Just reflect for a while and wipe the tears from your eyes. Always remember that you are loved and not alone. Clear the cobwebs from your mind as we guide you in your search for happiness and serenity.

Your quest for brilliance and lightness of spirit will soon come to an end for we will help you reconnect and reconcile with the Universe. You are about to embark on an incredible journey of self-discovery and success mastery.

We will help you transcend all emotions that caused you pain and misery. You will soon forget your constant struggles to meet your daily needs. You will find doors of opportunities opening to you which were locked before, despite your incessant knocking. You will be awed by the outpouring of blessings that would come your way.

From now on, stop blaming yourself for your inadequacies and shortcomings. You are a beautiful creation of God and deserve all the accolades and miracles that we will pour on you. You will finally recognize the unique and creative person that you truly are.

And now, as you reflect on the words we have imparted to you, we will await your transformation as we travel with you on your journey of illumination to be One, at last, with the Universe.

Let your inner glow shine brightly as you realize your passion and manifest your dreams. Prepare your heart and mind to receive the countless blessings we are about to pour on you.

Listen and be blessed.

The Universe

Today is your birthday, for the gift that I am about to share with you is a blueprint of an amazing transformation that will bring you immense joy and relief from the abyss that you have plunged yourself into. I will remove the blinders from your eyes and show you immense possibilities that will help in the realization of your dreams ... a gift that will re-establish your connection with the Divine and reconcile you with the Universe.

I congratulate you for taking the initiative to reach out and seek for the truth that has eluded you all this time. You will soon realize that the answers to your prayers lie within yourself, deeply hidden and unreachable until you remove the layers of armor which you have inadvertently worn for self-preservation and dignity.

I was not always like this. I was once like you, lost in the quagmire of misery, wallowing in self-pity, plagued by seemingly endless challenges financially and emotionally ... losing my job, my house and my husband all at the same time. I constantly blamed others for my inner turmoil and constant struggles as I faced a bleak future of loneliness and despair.

It was so easy for me to put the blame on somebody else, never recognizing the part I played to bring about these terrible consequences. And then I realized that these hardships were brought on by my erratic behavior and wrong decisions. I was so trusting of anyone who came to me, taking advantage of my generosity and pure intentions. Had I listened to my inner voice, I would not have experienced the downward spiral that put me in this desperate situation.

Out of the abyss, hope was born. I realized that I had to experience failure so I can bask in the glow of my success as I stepped into the deepest secrets of the Universe. I woke up and fought to survive for I knew that I deserved to live a better and more peaceful life. Hence, I found the strength within myself to overcome these challenges and finally align myself with the Universe.

Yet incredibly I never lost faith, never lost trust in God that someday He will relieve me of the burden that I had inadvertently laid on my shoulders. And then when I felt that there was no way out, the Universe suddenly opened and showed me my limitless potential.

I enjoin you to follow me as I show you the step-by-step guide to finally achieve a life full of happiness, love and success.

STEP-BY-STEP GUIDE TO HAPPINESS AND SUCCESS

1. Acceptance of the Situation
2. Surrender Completely
3. Forgive Yourself and Others

4. Desire to Change
5. Unclutter Your Mind
6. Be Grateful for Everything
7. Know What You Want
8. Make a Soul Intention
9. Believe in Yourself
10. Always have Faith and Trust in God
11. Take Action
12. Spread Love
13. Be Happy

1. ACCEPTANCE OF THE SITUATION

First of all, you have to recognize the depth of the situation that you have inadvertently sank into. You have to know the events that led you into this hopeless despair.

You have to accept the role that you unconsciously played that has brought about untold chaos in your life, whether financial, emotional or otherwise. Some people are in denial and go through life trudging along. They have given up their right to be part of this big beautiful world which the Universe has provided for us.

You should realize that this seemingly desperate situation is just temporary. When you are really down, there is no other way to go but up. You have to accept that you can no longer solve it by yourself and that you need the Universe to turn everything around for you.

2. SURRENDER COMPLETELY

Now is the best time to reach out to the Universe and completely surrender all the troubles that are bothering you.

As you pray and face our Creator, lift all your troubles to Him, whatever they may be. Plead with Him, cry if you must, and raise up your arms to Him. Tell Him that the load you are carrying is so heavy that you surrender everything to Him.

You have to tell Him that you have tried your best and yet the load seemed heavier as the days passed. Unload all your insecurities, pain and troubles up to Him.

It is time to let go and surrender completely.

3. FORGIVE YOURSELF AND OTHERS

Stop blaming yourself for your wrong choices and bad decisions. They have already happened and should never be repeated. It is time to forgive yourself as well as all the other people whom you think have done you wrong.

Unless you forgive from your heart, you will still be harboring bitterness and resentment which would just prevent you from manifesting what you want. Before you can reconcile with the Universe you first have to reconcile with yourself and others, with your family and friends for that matter.

Go ahead ... tell the Universe that you have finally stopped playing the victim. Tell the Universe that you have now accepted your role in the scheme of things. Show the Universe that you totally remove the blame on yourself and others and that you forgive everyone including yourself with all your heart and soul.

At this point you will feel lightness of spirit for having done such benevolent act. You are indeed a beautiful creation of God.

4. DESIRE TO CHANGE

Develop a sense of urgency knowing that time is a precious commodity that would never come back. There is no use in crying over spilled milk.

Now is the best time to realize that it is never too late to pick up the pieces and move on, no matter how swamped and overwhelmed you are with a multitude of problems.

Find the strength within you to finally make a stand to change for the better. Recognize the fact that unless you do something today, you will never get out of the mess you are in.

Feel the change in you now as your heart beats much faster with renewed vigor towards the pursuit of your dreams and your soul's yearnings.

5. UNCLUTTER YOUR MIND

The blows that life had dealt you with has left you with a lot of doubts and fears that have lodged in your subconscious mind. From now on, do not let any negative thought disturb your mind. You have to realize that before any positive thought could occupy your mind, you have to release all these beliefs and habits that have limited your potential and which have accumulated as you grew to adulthood.

It will not be easy to remove these limiting habits and beliefs, but as you pour water into yourself imagine all these toxic thoughts being washed away by every drop of water that touches your body. You have to fill your mind with positive uplifting thoughts before you can proceed.

6. BE GRATEFUL FOR EVERYTHING

As you wake up in the morning be thankful for having seen the light filtering through your bedroom window, for hearing the traffic across the street, smelling the aroma of fresh coffee and sipping its rich flavor.

Be thankful for each and every failure that touched your life, for without them, you wouldn't feel the immense joy of triumph over your challenges.

Be grateful for all things, big or small, good or bad. Be thankful for the obstacles strewn on your path, for they have made you determined and inspired to be the best that you can be.

7. KNOW WHAT YOU WANT

At this point in time you must have already opened a portal with which you have re-established your connection to the Universe. You should dig deep inside yourself and ask what do you really want, what is your innermost desire. What wakes you up in the morning?

Are you happy with your present job or do you want to change jobs where your talents can be more appreciated and be put to good use?

Is your passion entirely different from your present career?

Once you know what you want, then visualize it … feel it … smell it … for you are now aligned with the Universe which has put all your desires in vibrational escrow.

8. MAKE A SOUL INTENTION

From the deepest recesses of your heart and soul write down not only what you intensely desire, but why you want it so desperately. In this way, the Universe will bring you untold blessings which even you cannot dare imagine.

9. BELIEVE IN YOURSELF

You are a magnificent creation of God. You are unique in your individuality and you possess all the qualities and abilities necessary to help manifest your dreams. You are the only one who can turn your life around. Be confident and stay focused.

10. ALWAYS HAVE FAITH AND TRUST IN GOD

Remember to keep your faith and trust in God. It is this spiritual connection which helps us transcend all negative emotions. God never fails to deliver on His promises.

11. TAKE ACTION

Once you know what you want and have set your soul intention, you have to take action towards achieving your goals. You have to learn or study about the goals you have set and what needs to be done, and then shift your mind towards its realization. When you decide to take action, you create a powerful energy or a magnet that will attract manifold blessings and bring your goals closer to you.

12. SPREAD LOVE

This step is crucial. The Universe has decided to help you to manifest your dreams. It is imperative that you share such unconditional love to the people around you. Touch their lives the way the Universe touched yours. This is called paying it forward. By doing this, you help spread universal love that would one day create a world where people live in compassion, humility, peace and harmony.

13. BE HAPPY

This is the last step towards success mastery. By learning to adapt a cheerful countenance, the energy around you will shift towards positivity and a lot of possibilities. Once you exude this happiness from within yourself, you will keep on attracting immense rewards and blessings from the Universe.

Dearly beloved,

We commend you for embarking on this journey of self-discovery. We have seen your remarkable transformation and congratulate you.

You have managed to wipe your slate clean and reconcile with us.

We are now going to pour on you unimaginable rewards and blessings for your sacrifices and patience.

Remember always that we love you tremendously and expect you to reach out and spread compassion, humility and, most importantly, unconditional love.

Let love and peace reign in your hearts and may you stand united in this wonderful circle of light towards enlightenment.

The Universe

About Dr. Joyce

Dr. Edna Joyce C. Santos, MD, DPBO, SBO is an accomplished and dedicated ophthalmologist for the past 27 years. She has pioneered the establishment of the Southern Tagalog Society of Ophthalmology for which she had received numerous citations and awards for various eye missions during her term as President. She was also the Past President of the Philippine Medical Women's Association, Lucena-Quezon Chapter, for four years. She had shown remarkable competence and professionalism as Head of the Department of Ophthalmology in different hospitals in her country and in the United Arab Emirates. She is also sought after as international speaker in her field of expertise.

At this point in time of her career she has found her passion in writing. She has found it fulfilling to be able to touch people's lives and share her thoughts and feelings with the world. Despite her success in her career, for which she is truly grateful, she has not been spared a life of frustrations and anxieties – emotionally and financially. This is where she draws her motivation to tell people that they matter … that they are truly and incredibly loved by the Universe.

Dr. Joyce has various books out for publication soon, including her biography, *Are You Crazy?*, as well as the biography of Wolfgang Christoff, *Sohni*, who, by the way, is her life coach in her personal journey to life transformation. She will have a follow up to her book which would delve into her incredible journey to finally find pure and genuine love, peace and harmony in her life. She has found inspiration in her daughter, Pauline, and the unconditional love of a man who stood by her, cried with her and believed in her incredible abilities and great capacity to love. She is thankful to her friends who believed in her and showed her what a remarkable human being she truly is.

She is presently the official spokesperson and liaison officer for Miss Sophia Stewart, world famous author and franchise holder of *The Matrix Trilogy* and *Terminator* series. Watch out for the movie, *The Matrix 4*, and its attractions, as well as follow up sequels for the same.

She is a staunch advocate of human rights and would not hesitate to be the voice of the underdog when called upon. She is also an avid environmentalist.

Dr. Joyce is eternally grateful for all the blessings the Universe has poured on her and would like to be an inspiration to the world to make it a better place to live in.

She is a psychologist as well, and an active student of life, ever curious, ever evolving. Come and be a part of her amazing journey.

Dr. Joyce can be contacted via:
- Email: drfatimaedna2015@gmail.com
- LinkedIn.com/in/dr-edna-joyce-santos-426125a6, and
- Skype: fatima.joyce1

CHAPTER 18

THE ORCHESTRATED PARADIGM OF STORY INTO TRUTH

BY NINA M. KELLY

Life is a symbiotic journey of a thousand miles as we attempt to identify our true direction and find creative success from our discovered passion. For many years, I failed to recognize that my own mastery could be found in the united power of story and healing. Although I had spent my personal and professional existence enthusiastically listening to stories, it had never occurred to me that the power of the story was indeed my lifeline – it was my mastery.

As a child, my personal code of integrity was galvanized by the stories my mother told. Listening to them, I understood her desire for the evolution of human kindness, and the unequivocal love for humanity she expressed through service offered with compassion and acceptance. Then, when I was only seven, my mother suddenly died. I remember being outside, at night, playing hide-and–seek in the yard, when the minister's car pulled up. We ran over to it, and he brought us inside and told us the shocking story of my mother's death – not a story I wanted to hear, but one that ultimately sent me on a new involuntary journey. I began the search for healing. I wished to replace the excruciating pain of loss with the energy of life. Naturally, as a child, you want to see everything alive and vibrant with the capacity for interaction, with the living ability to share. Fate, however, offered me the exact opposite; my life seemed shadowed by the presence of death. Soon I learned that life and death are simply one breath away. They dance ever so closely together. This knowledge sharpened my vision and helped me become acutely aware of the undeniable role that story plays in healing.

Year after year, I witnessed many scenarios in which, if I carefully listened, I could hear the heart speak through words or actions. With time, I understood that the heart, the life force of all human creation, would not remain silent. It told its story through voice, music, graphic art, dance, through any or all of the applied or performed arts. I found myself working first with dying patients, then organ donations and transplantation. I witnessed these physically-fragile people needed to express their stories. They eagerly searched for outlets for their painful experiences and reflections on life – a need driven by an imperative to find that their lives had meaning and purpose. They felt an urge to share and open their hearts at the most vulnerable of times despite immense wounds. Such were the richness of stories that they have the capacity to heal the emotionally wounded, the physically injured, and the psychologically traumatized, while also healing communities. Watching people recover from illnesses, I saw that a capacity to heal the self originates deep in the heart, in the stories it needs to tell.

Again and again, I found myself sitting at the bedside of dying patients and witnessing a slight twinkle in their eyes as they expressed deeply-hidden memories, recalled with great sincerity in hopes of finding meaning. Soon the light would be extinguished in those eyes, but always the story lived on.

After many years of embracing others' stories, it finally came to my full awareness that the remembrance of the power that is held within a story was what I needed for my personal evolution. I felt it ring true that my individual mastery, my true success, could be found in the voice of story. It became clearer than ever that, for me, continued personal success in life meant sharing the many healing stories I had been honored to witness. My gift had been within me all along, in the wellspring of the narrative, the voice of story. Having absorbed the teachings of many masters who impart the wisdom of opening our hearts to receive, I was ripe to understand an obvious truth within myself. There is the storyteller, and the listener, and there is also a third, unknown presence who connects the giver and the receiver in order to bring forth healing.

Many experiences in my past attest to the importance of story as it relates to living and dying. My many years in private nursing came first, while I furthered my education. During that period, I learned that the fabric for story resides in every individual and merely awaits an invitation to express itself.

I had the opportunity to work with terminal patients and listen to their stories over the course of many hours. Realizing that sharing their stories was a necessary part of completing their lives brought to my awareness their acute need to be heard. In fact, allowing the venue to tell one's story was often more therapeutic than any other form of treatment for the terminal patient. I heard the angst of grief and loss, the elation of happiness and love, and almost every other emotion imaginable. Even as the patient became weaker, their passionate embrace of a particular portion of their life continued to shine through the meager remainder of their life force. The physical body was frail, but their story was filled with life.

As the body weakened, the mind often turned to philosophic expressions as a way to share feelings and experiences that had remained hidden inside for years. In the face of death, many patients felt a need to offer pearls of wisdom, to share the ways their life experiences had molded their life paths, perhaps, even contributing in some small way to their current state of affairs. Whether or not the dying patients realized it, they offered a gift to anyone who was willing to listen, to hear. Even so, their last words were often of appreciation that someone heard their voice. This taught me a valuable lesson: story is a gift that can be given most freely. Even if the patient could not recover physically, the mere act of giving voice to their story allowed healing to occur on a spiritual or emotional level. The final narrative prepared a peaceful home in which they could rest.

When my journey took me to work with organ procurement, my vision expanded. Patients declared brain dead became potential vascular organ donors for the critical patients that have the desire to continue living. These vascular donors offered the individuals a true gift of life. The loss of one's life offers the unconditional "gift of life" to an unknown person. That is the definition of true beauty. One relinquishes life and brings renewed existence to another – the gift given to the transplant patient who is praying for the opportunity to continue to live. To this day, the stories of these exchanges resonate within my being. It is difficult to comprehend: losing the one you love most and in that same moment giving another life. I repeatedly witnessed grieving family members, at the most tragic time, offer an unknown person sincere charity of the heart.

Over and over again, the healing that grieving family members experienced was profound. Later they shared their stories of how that gift had helped them heal. The loss of their loved one did not seem to be in vain, but instead, a continuation of life. Witnessing this restores one's belief in the resilience of the human spirit and the core truth that everyone shares a sense of meaning in life; expressed or not.

Each time I listened to the passion in the story of another, I recognized they had the power to heal simply by expressing their story. It need not be the voice; they could have the same effect through a different medium. The profound power of expression through the art form of stories, continues to enrich my understanding of life. I am grateful that my experience with Jack Canfield, Steve Harrison and the entire team, reinforced the clarity in understanding my journey, and encouraged me to continue with the vision and the belief that the creation of stories can bring forth both physical and psychological healing.

Understandably, the expression of feelings in stories prepare the foundation for healing. Allowing one to have a voice is an undeniable gift, an act of courtesy, and potentially much more. It is a reciprocal event in which the listener offers to receive, in return for being given that which is shared from another's heart.

How exciting to suggest a revisited paradigm of healing, one in which the patient creates the story of love originating from the heart. The human heart is the vital vascular organ without which we cannot live. Since stories originate from this essential organ, therein lies the potential for human compassion to flourish and for everyone to create the imaginative healing story that they can implement to cure their sufferings.

This brings us to the realm of children and how powerful their imaginations become when given the freedom of expression. Children, with their great capacity for relating to images, are masters at creating stories of love and healing. And using this instrument of creativity, their emotional and physical infirmities may be healed. With all the healing modalities implemented in modern medicine, I see a place for yet another; to envision stories and images bringing healing to children. How wonderful to witness young ones learning how to find the power of their voices and to deliver themselves stories that heal. This is my vision of a new paradigm shift in consciousness. What an incredible spark to add to life.

Currently, I am working with an illustrator, Lawrence Fothe, on such a project. How phenomenal to imagine a mythical tale in which little children become so self–empowered that they can identify a new pathway toward healing wherein they are the maestros of their orchestrated personal creations?

What better tool than the power of story?

About Nina

Nina M Kelly is a mythologist with an emphasis in depth psychology, storytelling, author, humanitarian, and cultural and arts activist. She also is an Archetypal Pattern Analyst and Dream Pattern Analyst. Nina's sense of adventure has always been sparked through learning more about people and their cultures. Believing that if you understand a person's culture, stories, myths, and rituals, then you more readily open your world to greater compassion.

Her passion for the art of healing through stories brought her to the place of writing *Grace Has A Silent Voice*, where she honors the silent heroes and the resilience of the human spirit. Working with death and dying patients, she acquired a tremendous respect for the proper honoring of story. In her book, she acknowledged the silent heroes that walk into our lives for a moment then quickly disappear. This inevitably leaves an imprint that continues to remind us that there is beauty in humanity.

Nina's doctorate is from Pacifica Graduate Institute in Mythological Studies and Emphasis on Depth Psychology, and her dissertation research was completed through Louisiana State University Medical Center in New Orleans, Louisiana. Dissertation: *Myth Making and Modern Medicine, A Case of Kidney Transplantation*. Her research work included reducing the rejection episodes post-transplant, implementing the power of stories and images. She published *The Lost Heritage* in Psychology at the Threshold.

Nina is also an Archetypal Pattern Analyst and Dream Pattern Analyst where she completed her studies from Assisi International Institute and published, *Weaving Story Into The Web*.

As an executive film producer for the short film, *Dandelion*, the film won the judges award and has been shown at several film festivals. She has also served as president of the New Orleans Opera Association, president of Southern Repertory Theatre, Chair for Loyola University School of Music Visiting Committee, president and CEO of the Children's Bureau, publishing the history of the Children's Bureau, *Saving Wednesday's Child*, authored by Mark Cave, and authoring the introduction and acknowledgements. Throughout her tenure, she has served on numerous non-profits boards.

Nina continues to challenge us through the inspiration and motivation of storytelling. She continues to believe that the art form of storytelling and story sharing originate from the heart of everyone searching for expression – thus healing both listener and teller.

You may contact Nina at:
- Nina@ninastime.com
- www.ninamkelly.com

CHAPTER 19

WHEN THE RUBBER MEETS THE ROAD

BY RITA DUNHAM

For unto whomsoever much is given,
of him shall be much required.
~ Luke 12:48 (KJV)

The purpose of this chapter is to help anyone who is going through a struggle of any kind to overcome some of life's most difficult challenges and still achieve their goals – through words of encouragement and life experience. A lot of people have no idea what it feels like to lose practically everything and spend years in the trenches of life – on life's terms and conditions. Then, there are those of us who do. I call it, *"When the rubber meets the road."*

It's that desperation point between what we feel like we deserve in life and what we're actually *getting*. If you know what it's like to struggle or are in a dark place of pain, lack or any type of human suffering…this chapter's for you. And just know that you are NOT alone. At some point we all experience setbacks, roadblocks and disappointments. Our experiences train - teach – and ultimately MAKE or BREAK us. Wisdom is not automatically given. It has to be _earned_. And sometimes the pitfalls in our life can last so long and run so deep that they cloud our perception of reality, causing us to feel that there is no way out.

In March of 2011, after several hours of grueling surgeries, my husband and father of my children succumbed to an inoperative brain tumor and our oldest child's Autism had spiraled into an aggressive life-threatening condition. I had to quit my job, drop out of school and postpone all of my writing and real estate endeavors to take care of my family.

In a matter of months, I went from having a thriving marriage and family, a fulfilling teaching career, the brink of entrepreneurship and pursuing my Master's in Education – to a broken widow putting flowers on my husband's grave, dropping 'Fat Boy' off at the local dog pound and packing up my entire household. SOLO! And I had to relocate what was left of me and my two children (a daughter in such a haze of aggression, it could have shamed the 'Karate Kid', and a son who could count to almost a thousand since the age of five, disassemble any kind of electrical gadget known to man – including cable, his high chair, set timers, reboot computers, spell almost anything in the dictionary from A through Z and an Honor Roll recipient every year – but still struggled to communicate at his appropriate grade level) all on my *own*.

I had NO job, NO support, and NO HOPE. Talk about a wake-up call *and* a sucker punch? There were definitely days that I DID NOT WANT to get out of bed. BUT I KNEW I HAD TO. I kept thinking, *"This is all just a crazy nightmare. Eventually I'm bound to wake up."* Unfortunately, the alarm clock just never seemed to go off. I couldn't fathom how to even *begin* to get back up. The only reading on my radar was LOST, STUCK, and DEFEATED. In my weakest hour, I had to be stronger than I ever had to be in my entire life. With not only one – but THREE souls depending on me ... including my own.

I found myself in an extremely dark place with no one to lean on or to understand my trial. And from that day forth, I promised myself if I ever made it out of that dark tunnel, I would try my best to help someone else who is going through a similar experience and feels like there is no place to turn – because I know what that's like. One of my passions is sharing my message and bits of my journey through my writing in hopes of breathing life and encouragement into someone else's situation – my faith and refusal to give up is what has kept me during the storm. My hope is that one day my vision will manifest in a way that will greatly enrich the lives of others.

Here are my ten steps for achieving your goals despite your struggles:

Step 1 – *Seize Control*
Eventhough the curveballs of life can sometimes besiege us with undesirable circumstances outside our control, the fact still remains that it is our responsibility to clean up the wreckage – regardless of how it got there. We must be willing to roll up our sleeves and do the work in order to 'seize control' and take back our life.

Step 2 – *Ride the Tide*
I always knew there was more to life *than the life I was living*. I wanted to get out but just didn't know how. Sometimes when we are thrust into a dark place it is necessary, at least in my case, I had to actually date my struggle, become one with it, and get to know its strengths and weaknesses – and pull from my inner strength in order to learn how to diffuse it. I had to stop running from it and face it head-on. Underestimating the power of my struggle became too expensive, and I could no longer afford to let it pull me under or it would continue to steal even more years of my life. We all have an inner voice that will guide us to safety if we are still enough to hear it. A story very close to my heart is that of a woman who found herself in the middle of a tsunami in a make-shift floating device from the debris of the storm. She told the reporter that just as a huge surge of waves headed in her

direction and she was about to go under, instinct told her to ride the tide rather than resist it, and the current that could have easily taken her under actually ended up carrying her to safety.

Step 3 – *Patience is a Virtue*
Desire without action will never create success. It takes work when it comes to accomplishing our goals. Rarely do they come overnight – especially when we're dealing with or coming back from a setback. There have been countless times when I have struggled so long and saw very minimal to no results from my efforts. I felt like I was running on a hamster's wheel. We all have experienced times and circumstances where we feel like just throwing in the towel and running for the hills.

For years, my family lived in crisis mode from my daughter's struggle with Autism and the lack of funding for therapeutic services that would have made a world of difference in my child's life. I was at the end of my rope many times when I looked at the direction my life had taken, despite all my hard work, quitting my job and bearing the prognosis of my husband's illness. Then one day it came to me. ... Almost like a revelation.

During some of the most difficult times in my life, the only way I overcame them was by digging my heels in even deeper – going deeper even when it seemed like the situation was only getting worse. . . when we feel broken beyond repair. I overcame by pressing on while waiting, while struggling and often while crying. The only thing that hurts more than giving up is giving up after giving your all or quitting right before your breakthrough. No matter how hard it gets, there is no life in quitting. But there is one definite guarantee – if you give up, you will NEVER achieve success!

Step 4 – *One-Upping Fate*
Whenever I am facing any type of challenge, setback or loss, I believe it is imperative to put something positive back into my life to offset the momentum of failure and keep things on an

even keel. Instead of just allowing the unpredictable winds of life to carry us any and everywhere, sometimes we need to even the score, and there is nothing more rejuvenating than conquering a new adventure.

Step 5 – *Disciplined Consistency*
Discipline and consistency go hand in hand when it comes to achieving success at any magnitude. Without dedication and the constant drive to remain committed to your goals, it is nearly impossible to achieve them. In my experience, whenever my circumstances seem to be consistently working directly against whatever I am trying to accomplish – it is crucial that I match the challenge with an equal level of consistency or higher, in order to overcome the barrier of whatever it is that is holding me back. I call it 'Tactical Combat.'

Step 6 – *Taking Risks*
My first real estate deal was quite…scary…to be perfectly honest. I grew up observing and learning the ins and outs in various sectors of the business from several family members. But over time, through death and relocation, many of those family members were no longer there for me to glean their advice. So, when it came down to *my very first transaction* … I was once again standing on my own. After months of looking at several properties and finally setting sights on one in particular and doing the math, there were a lot of major reasons to deter me from cutting the deal.

The start-up investment, cost of material, labor and an endless search for trustworthy contractors in a seriously fickle market was a HUGE risk. The looming possibility of investing in something that might not sell and possibly cause me a ton of trouble down the line or worse – no ROI (Return On Investment) – not to mention I could lose *everything* I had, kept me up at night long after signing on the dotted line. Eventually I had to come to the realization that there was no way I would ever gain any experience, knowledge or success in the real estate market without taking some risks. They should be preferably calculated but that was not always possible. I had to put the fear of risk taking to bed – once and for all.

Step 7 – *The Nay-Sayers*
I, personally, have experienced *more* than my fair share of criticism. It actually propelled me to go back to school and get my degree, undertake the real estate market, write novels, columns…even teach. In life, you will always encounter critics. No matter what you do and regardless of how good or how bad you do it – there will be those with an opinion. There is a distinct difference between constructive criticism and negative feedback. It takes a certain amount of skill to turn 'shade' into fossil fuel.

I like to ask myself three questions when I know I'm being criticized. Is it true? Does the gossiper have my best interest at heart? What is this individual doing in their own life to make a positive contribution on this planet before their time is up? Most critics will usually go away once they realize all the time they are wasting as the person they are judging is actually setting and achieving actual goals. Sometimes you just have to 'believe in you' and give *yourself* a high-five, instead of waiting on someone else to do it.

Step 8 – *Maintaining*
At one point I was so laden with grief and stress that I re-engaged with my faith and decided to go talk to a pastor. After intently listening to me he told me something that would change my life forever, *"If it hasn't taken you out yet, then it doesn't have authority over you."* It is imperative when you are going through to connect with people who will support you, encourage you and are wiser than you are. People who have more life experience than we do can offer so much wisdom. Everyone needs and DESERVES a support system.

In this world, there is always a 'cause-and-effect' in relation to our actions. And while the world doesn't bend to our needs, there are so many ways we can invite peace back into our lives just by the way we treat people. We can never build our happiness on someone else's pain. If we are mindful on our journey, we can achieve the unimaginable. Everyone has pain in their life, but it's how you deal with the pain that makes the ultimate difference.

Step 9 – *Giving Back (to You)*
Reaching out to help someone else is one of the most therapeutic experiences I have ever had when going through my own difficulties. It's a good feeling when you can actually encourage someone else along the way even when you are struggling. And just as there is a time and a season for everything under the sun, there is also a time to stop to celebrate and acknowledge your own achievements, your victories, your pain and your journey. Don't be so hard on yourself. Sometimes we are often our own worst critics. *Take time to give yourself a break and by doing so you will be giving yourself a chance.*

Step 10 – *Conclusion*
It is important to remember that the steps we need to take back control of our lives take time, self-assessment and courage. There is a certain level of discipline needed to also maintain the changes you have put into place when restructuring your life. It is not a quick fix – but a lifestyle change.

There IS a light at the end of the tunnel. We just have to remain steadfast enough in our journey to push through in order to bask in the rays of its brilliance.

About Rita

Rita Dunham is a single mom, educator, novelist and real estate investor. She has also worked in various capacities within the field of writing.

In her spare time, she enjoys spending time with her children, working out and taking long strolls along the beach. One of her key missions in life is to inspire others through her writing by sharing bits of her journey in hopes of empowering those who may be going through a struggle, with a message that there is always HOPE.

CHAPTER 20

KEEP YOUR EYES ON THE PRIZE
STAYING FOCUSED THROUGH THE INTERRUPTIONS OF SUCCESS

BY KATRINA EARLY

There will always be some force trying to deter us from achieving our God-given purpose. Why not make it a stepping stone instead of a roadblock?

Everything that has happened to me in my life has driven me in some way. I wasn't afraid of hard work or proving to anybody that I was more than what they said. So imagine my surprise when I achieved "success" as most people define it, and it wasn't all I'd built it up to be.

My career was soaring and people noticed. I received numerous awards and honors, all things that showed how what I was doing was appreciated by someone. It seemed that to everyone else, my life was ideal. But to me, something was missing.

Everything happening in my life forced me to evaluate why I was empty inside when my life seemed to be so filled with rewards.

I was so confused by what I was not feeling and knew that I had to seek out the reason(s) for my discontentment, and then resolve them. Through this process, I never imagined the challenges that I would meet that really put me to the test, and brought me to a place where I could realize my full potential, despite the constant interruptions.

INTERRUPTION OVERLOAD

*I committed to a spiritual journey that I felt would be
Representative of what God had in mind for my destiny.*

The first part of my spiritual journey was a commitment to celibacy. I'd had my son when I was in my very early twenties, and had never been married to his father. Despite having faith and being connected to God, I wasn't acting in the way that He states we should through His teachings and the Bible. By making this simple commitment as a grown woman, I already began to feel my self-worth.

My attention turned to how I could help and serve others, and that was when Make Me Mold Me Empowerment, Inc. was formed. This was a concept that would allow me to reach out to women and empower them to reach their God-given potential in a nurturing and positive manner.

*Everyone can achieve their God-given potential,
regardless of where they begin their journey at.*

As I focused on teaching, I was being freed from bondage and the ladies were being inspired. The space that had been a void inside of me was quickly filling up with faith and a new kind of love for the world I lived in, and what I could do for it.

Things only got better when I met a man that I felt connected with. I was certain that God had brought him my way and I was overjoyed. After two years of dating on and off, we finally decided to get married. My new life was beginning…only it turned out to be far from my expectations. Two challenging, faith-testing things happened:

1. After only being married two weeks, my husband told me he wanted a divorce so he could go back to his child's mother.
2. I learned I had breast cancer.

I'd been doing everything I could, so how could this happen? It was the ultimate test. Would I be able to walk in faith and belief, or would I feel that I'd been abandoned by God, despite striving to have a relationship with him?

FROM TRIAL TO TESTIMONY

Doing the right thing during challenging times is a true test to our commitment and faith.

Learning that what I thought was a God-given marriage was really an abusive and degrading one was shocking. Knowing I had cancer was an insecure feeling. I had to make a choice— either defeat these things or have them defeat me. If everything I'd practiced and professed over the years was authentic, I had no reason to worry. This is the approach I took, as I felt it in my heart. The moment and time I was in was during my trial, and I had to seek the lessons that existed within it, even if they made no sense to me. After all, they still had a purpose or God wouldn't have placed them there.

I was given an opportunity to grow even stronger through the personal controversies and struggles in my life.

The enemy was coming at me from two different directions. With my husband, I had to deal with the degrading way he treated me now and looked at me. He'd tell me how unappealing I was because of my scars and I truly sensed he was waiting for me to break. Then I had to address the cancer itself, and I was so determined to not allow it to take over my mind, body, and soul. Managing this meant that I had to keep my eyes on the prize, and learn what I could from every experience I had.

For starters, the only power I was going to hand over was to God himself. If I would have given even a fraction of it away to my husband or the cancer, my outcome might be different. Today's testimony wouldn't be the same, if it even existed.

In the end, I was victorious. I was able to separate from the relationship that there was a path on my way to what God had designed for me, and I also walked away from cancer – a woman in remission. My scars are reminders of my victory fought with the gentle, loving hands of the Lord.

Today, I use these lessons to offer my testimony of how walking on the right path can take us to places we would never choose on our own. I'm able to show other women that no matter what they go through, they have one task: to keep their eyes on God and not allow the situation to overtake them. They must overtake the situation!

THE VICTORY IN PERSEVERANCE

Let God close the doors behind you and guide you
to your next door that will open.

When I became free of cancer and my abusive husband, I was liberated to continue on my journey towards my greater purpose. There was still work to do, because I had to let go of the things that were holding me back. I had to reconcile my faith with the reality of what I often thought about, which was how humiliating it was for a professional, well-known woman in my community to be with an abusive husband and go through the cancer I had. The answer was to release my ego and share the experience. There were so many people that I could help, and it turned out that my victory could be their inspiration.

About this time I received another award—a lifetime achievement award from my community. This was the most special award, not because I needed acknowledgement from anyone about what I'd done, but because it represented the results of my faith and conviction in action.

Then, four months after my divorce, God introduced me to the man I'd dreamt about years ago. The one that was a gift to me, from Him. It was Demetrius and I knew my time was right to walk a journey in faith with someone else who'd had their own challenges. He'd been promised to me and I was finally in a place where I could acknowledge that I was ready to have him come to me.

My family and friends tried to dissuade me about my now-husband daily, but I had no doubts about what we could do together.

Demetrius was a God-fearing and loving husband, lifting me up and helping me gain clarity in the few areas of my life where I still struggled. Sadly, it was with my family. I'd never addressed the problems of my childhood and adult life with them before. Nothing I ever did was good enough, and they thought me foolish to leave the abuser in the first place. When I gravitated toward Demetrius they came at me in a negative force that was only protected by God's good grace for me. Demetrius was bold, protective, and supportive, and he also helped me to see the truth in my mother and sister. Those two had been particularly cruel about letting me know that I was no longer welcome in their life, because I was "a nothing" and "brainwashed." Verbally, my mother and sister expressed their dislike for me and my husband, and advised me to go on with my life in Shreveport. So I did. And I thank everyone for helping guide me to that pivotal decision.

Sometimes, a verbal slap in the face is just what we need to wake up and turn on the light so we can see the truth.

My life instantly became better, because while family is important, blood ties cannot be stronger than our ties with God and purpose—ever. I was comfortable with who I was and had forgiven my mistakes and forgave my family, too. I was finally released from a generational curse I ignored for years. I walked away, giving glory to God for my successes in life with a genuine heart and gratitude.

You see, once I accepted the truth, I was able to walk in it with dignity, and it was certainly easier than lying about the reality of what I'd willingly surrounded myself with for so long, things which were unhealthy for me. I figured that God didn't spare me from cancer just to bring me to a lie. I didn't go through the abusive marriage to heal me or make me lose my mind, but to show me how to truly love and forgive in the way God would.

IT'S NOT THE ISSUES – IT'S THE LESSONS

When you welcome a different viewpoint on your issues,
you can begin to view them from the eyes of the Maker.
This is when things change.

All those things that have interrupted my success for so long are now out of the way. Will something else arise in my life? Likely, that is part of life, but knowing that I've learned how to use the lessons as stepping stones to success helps me to not fear them. It's always exciting to reveal the mystery of God's plans for us.

People often ask me what feels different about the woman I am today, in comparison to the one I was when I had the "illusion of success." This is what I know to be true:

- I am honest with myself.
- I feel healed.
- Life is less scary.
- My thoughts and walk today give me a freedom I've never had before.

- I am not in the shadows of anything, but in the light of God.
- Because I walk with the man God has given me, it doesn't matter what others think and do. What this man wants me to do is remain true.

Life is all about what happens as a result of our freewill and the choices we make. And although we are in God's hands, we still have work to do in order to experience success and remove the interruptions that stop us along the way.

Here are seven reminders to help you when you find yourself in life situations that interrupt you and challenge you:

1. **Burst through the clouds of others' expectations.**
   What you expect of yourself and what God has in store for you are the only expectations that you need to meet. You don't have to be the failure that anyone else says you are, or an enabler of weakness.
2. **Understand the importance of self-determination.**
   Your results are a product of your choices. Be determined to craft your own destiny and not leave it in the hands of anyone else. Remember, God is your guide, but you take the action.
3. **When it's important, you will not fail to work your plan.**
   Our biggest struggles often come when we are forcing things to be right in our lives that just aren't. When something is aligned with our purpose and blessed by God, it's not a burden to work our plans out to completion.
4. **Let patience and faith be your guide.**
   It can be tough to believe this and act out on it, but things do not always happen in our time. If we have lessons that need to be learned before we reach our rewards, we're better served to believe they will happen, keep working to become stronger and better, and not lose hope.
5. **We are ultimately responsible for determining our worth.**
   Other people do not determine our value in life, and put limitations on what we can accomplish. When we lose sight

of ourselves by believing other peoples' negative thoughts, we are not honoring God, who made us just the way he wanted us to be.

6. The sun is always behind even the grayest sky.

If you look at the world around you and see the gloom and doom, but not your potential to burst through it, you're going to struggle. Close your eyes, pray, and feel the warmth of the light. It is always there.

7. Sever your ties with emotional clutter.

When people and situations hold you back, don't ever feel that is your lot in life, because it is not. You can separate from what doesn't serve your greater good and find peace with yourself in the process. This is a beautiful way to honor God.

Service is at the heart of what I do every day. In my career, I serve others and help them out with their insurance and financial needs. Through Make Me Mold Me Empowerment, Inc., I serve people who are struggling with unanswered questions and lack clarity in their paths. In my marriage, I am of service to my husband, just as he is to me. These are the ultimate rewards, and by not doing them, it would be doing a disservice to the ultimate one that I serve—God—therefore myself, too.

About Katrina

As a strong, independent business woman, Katrina Early works diligently to give back to the community that has supported her through the years. Her professional mission through her agency is to help people overcome the risks and struggles of everyday life, recover from the unexpected, and realize their dreams...as she has realized her own.

After graduating with a B.S. degree from Arkansas State University, Katrina accepted a job with State Farm Insurance Companies in 1995. Simultaneously, she began decades of service to her country as a reservist in the United States Army. Six years later, she was appointed a fully-licensed State Farm Agent and began running her own agency in South Shreveport, helping clients throughout Northern Louisiana with their insurance and financial needs.

While running her own business has kept her busy, she also found opportunities to give back in other ways. Katrina served as president of the Minority Business Council (2008), on the Central Vice President's Council in 2005, and as a member of the Greater Shreveport Chamber of Commerce. From 2009 to 2013, she worked on Louisiana's Workforce Commission, and in 2014, Shreveport Mayor Cedric Glover appointed Katrina to serve on the City Workforce Commission. She is also a proud member of Zeta Phi Beta Sorority, Inc.

In 2010, due to her passion to help women discover themselves, she founded Make Me Mold Me Empowerment, Inc. which officially organized January 15, 2015. Through it, Katrina and her husband provide guidance in self-development, goal planning, and leadership by sharing with fellow men and women their experience and life-lessons. She strives to motivate and help other women recognize their potential and live holistic lives.

Katrina is a recipient of the "2015 Lifetime Achievement Award" with the Greater Shreveport Chamber of Commerce, and presented as Queen of Krewe of Harambee for 2015-2016 Mardi Gras season. Over the years, she's received many accolades in recognition of her contributions, including: Business Woman of the Year, Business Person of the Year, African-American Achievement Award, two separate Small Business of the Year awards and

Athena Women's Nominate.

After 21 years of service, she retired from the Army, but continues her civilian work as a successful State Farm Agent and a Notary Public. Her commitment to customer service and the community as a whole helped grow her business. In 2015, she was asked to temporarily service a second State Farm office in Minden. Katrina, along with her teams at both State Farm locations, take great pride in their goal to provide knowledge, respect, and good service to each and every customer, which they so richly deserve. Katrina feels she is truly blessed in her life and career, recognition that came when she fully realized – "God is in Complete Control."

She is a proud and devoted wife to Demetrius Early, mother of six children and G-Ma KK of six grandchildren, including most recent grandson, Jace.

If you would like to learn more, you can reach her via:
- Website: KEARLYINSURANCE.COM
- Email: MAKEMEMOLDMEPOWER@GMAIL.COM
- LinkedIn: KATRINA EARLY
- Facebook: KATRINA EARLY